Perceptions of the Amish Way

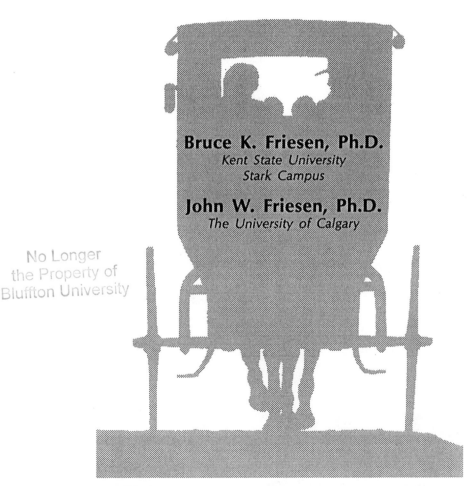

Bruce K. Friesen, Ph.D.
Kent State University
Stark Campus

John W. Friesen, Ph.D.
The University of Calgary

 KENDALL/HUNT PUBLISHING COMPANY
4050 Westmark Drive   Dubuque, Iowa 52002

To our Amish Cousins

Contents

Preface

The times, they are a changing, and the Amish are no exception. While the Old Order Amish community has always faced the threat of change, they have always adopted aspects of it, albeit usually on their own terms. Often the change has come about through external pressures, but from time to time members within the community have also augured for change, usually with regard to technological adaptations. As the population of North America continues to increase, means of transportation are enhanced, and interaction among the various cultural sectors of the continent is intensified, the Amish are finding it very difficult to maintain their separatist stance. As one Amish historian writes:

> . . . the Amish lost the ability to be fully private citizens, as each year their lives became the focus of attention for millions of interested and inquisitive visitors. Under careful eye and camera lenses, the Amish have become one of the most closely-examined people in America (Nolt, 1992, 277).

Perceptions of the Amish people vary greatly, as this volume will illustrate. The most positive, and probably naive perceptions of the Plain People, emanate from the tourist sector, influenced, no doubt by the colorful, alluring brochures manufactured by the business community in Amishland. According to these illustrative emissaries of potential financial gain, the Amish live an almost ideal lifestyle, capturing in totality the vitality and quiet beauty of the culture in early America. Unmolested by urban sprawl, pollution and crowding, the Amish are alleged to enjoy a daily routine of fresh air, family bonding, haystacks, buggy rides and horse-drawn farm implements. Small wonder that, having read the propaganda urging or implying that a return to the past will provide peace to the heart, tourists return again and again to Amishland to fantasize about the "good ole days". No amount of Amish mementoes, kerosene lamps, black bonnets or buggy rides in Amishland will bring the tourist any closer to what it means to be Amish. In some contexts this may prove to be a blessing.

To the more serious student of Amish ways, they represent the promise of autonomy, meaning and humaneness that are possible when the limitlessness of an atomic world is resisted. The Amish stand as a reminder that the deliberate imposition of limits is a constant struggle, not without its costs. While many North American citizens engage themselves in climbing the ladder to success by getting educated and striving for a raise or promotion, the Amish are busy trying to satisfy the requirements imposed upon them by their local church board. Their main concern is to fulfil and perpetuate the oracles and practices of their faith and transmit them to the next generation. Each potential influence or potential threat to existing cultural protocol must be approved by local church authorities whose role as adjudicators is continuous. Innovative technological gadgets perpetually rise up to lurk alluringly on the horizon of change to tempt the weaker members of the faith. When infractions occur, the process of investigation and judgment commence. Being taken to task for breaking the rules is an experience dreaded by every Amish person but it still occurs frequently in virtually every Amish congregation. It seems that few individuals, even if they are Amish, can totally avoid yielding to temptation in every situation.

In reality, the Amish are an example of a community who have very successfully striven for an independent lifestyle in the melting-pot milieu of American society. They have carefully and self-absorbedly integrated with dominant society almost exclusively on their own terms—with one or two exceptions. Their first clash with outside "interference" pertained to schooling, but some thirty years ago the Plain People won the battle to operate their own schools by action of the Supreme Court of the USA. The second outside invasion, that of technology, has been gradual but steady, and permitted if not encouraged by the Amish themselves. These developments are, for the most part, unknown to casual visitors in Amish country. Tourists are too impressed with the multiplicity of alluring items reflective of a colonial American-type culture which they may purchase and take home to remind themselves of their summer visit to a "country fantasyland".

A closer examination of Amish home life will reveal many distasteful characteristics from the perspective of the middle class American family. In Amish families, gender roles are generally quite clear. The husband is the head of the farm and the spiritual head of the family. Divorce is forbidden, and the feminist movement does not exist. The wife may rule the house, care for the children, and, on occasion, enjoy the fellowship of other Amish women during a quilt-making bee. Amish children are never left in a daycare because raising children is a sacred responsibility, just like caring for the land. Children are "an heritage of the Lord" (Psalm 127:3 KJV) and are to be desired. Traditionally, Amish families often included as many as ten children, although these numbers have decreased slightly in the last few decades. If the Amish are subject to the same kinds of pressures as their cousins, the Hutterites, there may be subtle developments that impinge on such matters as family size. Hutterite society has recently sired an underground women's movement which has resisted the tendency towards large families because some of their women have secretly begun to practice birth control without telling their husbands (Peter, 1987). Basically, it is still true among the Amish that if a women cannot have children she is not "blessed of the Lord" (Psalm 128:1-3 KJV). When blessed with children, the youngsters are to be raised with the admonition of the Lord. The central scriptural tenet revered by the Amish is,"Train up a child in the way that he should go, and when he is old he will not depart from it " (Proverbs 22:6). To the Amish that training, by the way, means total socialization into the Amish world.

As a successful cultural alternative to the mad, mad world of the microchip, the Amish have many admirers, but few joiners. One may wonder at this, because there is basically nothing to stand in the way of anyone wishing to head out to the green pastures of the countryside and establish a Daniel Boone-type lifestyle. One could even link up with a ready-made version of the good ole days and apply for membership with the Old Order Amish. Subject to minor conditions, this can be done, and through the three centuries of their existence a few have actually attempted to do this. According to at least one source, however, this route to bliss may encounter a few obstacles along the way. The greatest shock may be that these obstacles may materialize within the ranks of the hallowed sanctuary of Amishland.

The Life of a Convert

In 1969, Paul and Jan Edwards and their four children of Akron, Ohio, began life as members of an Old Order Amish congregation. Like many non-Amish the Edwards were disillusioned with the rat-race of middle-class urban life and sought to fulfil their search for a simpler, more peaceful way of life.

Following the Amish tradition of large families, the Edwards eventually had six additional children. Their experience in peaceful living lasted 17 years before the Edwards relocated to the middle-class urban life they had left behind, somewhat disillusioned by what they called a lack of acceptance by the Plain People. When they took their leave, the Edwards soon divorced, Mrs. Edwards and two of their children chose to remain in the Amish community. Paul Edwards has since remarried, his new wife, an Amish refugee. One of the family's ten Edwards' children, a son, even married a bishop's daughter. Then, following the Edwards family tradition of questioning things, he too was later excommunicated.

When the Edwards took up with the Amish they chose one of the more conservative, traditionally-oriented factions, namely the Swartzentruber sect. They served a probationary period of six years, learned the German language and gave up all "worldly" taboos such as electricity, skating, music, swimming and Christmas celebrations. As the years went by, however, they began to realize that the cultural shift they were experiencing was simply overwhelming. The gap between their old way of life and their fantasy world could not be surmounted. When they finally left the Swartzentruber people, like other Amish refugees, the Edwards shifted to a conservative Mennonite congregation, but the gap was still too great. The only realistic option was to return to dominant society (*The Independent*, July 10, 1995, C-5).

When members of the Amish community leave their particular community they tend to take up fellowship with a conservative Mennonite church, making the cultural gap for them to overcome, quite minor compared to that experienced by the Edwards family. The Edwards claimed that they were never accepted by their adoptive community, but frequently referred to by Amish insiders as "Englishmen". They were also disappointed to discover that the Swartzentruber People operated a school where the teacher meted out very harsh corporal punishment for infractions, and this was hard on their children. They discovered drugs, theft and alcohol abuse among Amish youth, and were hardly comforted by the thought that "the Amish are people too".

The Scholarly View

Although the Amish live in 22 different states and one Canadian province, their most publicized place of sojourn is Lancaster County, Pennsylvania, where 18,000 Amish make their home. While the Garden State draws its share of publicity about the Plain People, Holmes County, Ohio, actually has nearly twice as many Amish residents as Lancaster County. Still, it is Lancaster County that draws the greater portion of tourists, probably because they advertise more intensely for it. Thus when people think of Amish country, they usually think first of Lancaster County, Pennsylvania. There are 85 Amish districts in Lancaster County while Holmes County has 131 districts. The total number of Amish districts in North America is 227. At its present rate of growth, the Amish population will double every twenty years (Hostetler, 1993). If this rate of increase continues, it is quite likely that more states may eventually become hosts to new Amish congregations.

In July, 1993, 300 scholars from across North America, and several guests from other countries, gathered in Elizabethtown, Pennsylvania, to celebrate the 300th anniversary of the Old Order Amish. While no members of the Amish community attended the conference, a few participants who had formerly belonged to the Old Order joined in the program. For three days scholars presented speeches, exchanged scholarly papers and participated in other commemorative exercises. Dr. John A. Hostetler, internationally-known scholar on Amish sociology, was honored in a banquet for his literary contributions to Amish study. The fourth edition of Hostetler's book, *Amish Society*, was unveiled at the conference. The book first appeared in 1963, finally published by The Johns Hopkins University Press. Hostetler admitted to having tried more than a dozen publishers before the manuscript was accepted by The Johns Hopkins University Press. Most publishers turned down Hostetler's proposal on the basis that there was insufficient public interest in Amish study. Now, more than three decades later, Hostetler's book has sold more then 100,000 copies. Many North Americans, it seems, are interested in Amish society.

A Personal Note

This book offers a slightly different view of the Amish than most of the literature about the Plain People. It is written from a "cousin" perspective, both authors tracing their ancestry back to European Mennonite beginnings whose ancestors migrated to North America via Russia. This presentation is intended to be analytical, rather than venerating, basically with the intention of making the point that the Amish are people—just like us; they have their strong points and their failings. Amish people experience pain, cry, laugh and have good times. Observers should not be fooled by the tourist image of Amish buggies, bonnets and babies. Beneath their 17th century garments beats a human heart with the same desires and longings as that of any other human being. If the time should come that the Amish are finally perceived as "cousins to us all," instead of merely being the target of curiosity, we may begin to make some headway towards enhancing the meaning of cross-cultural interaction. Until that time the Amish way of life will remain a bit of an intriguing mystery, shrouded in the unfortunate trappings of contemporary tourist literature.

At this point we must necessarily thank a number of people for being supportive and assisting with this project, particularly the many Amish folk who have been kind enough to share stories about their way of life with us. Our wives, Deborah K. Zuercher Friesen and Virginia Lyons Friesen, have been supportive and critical (in a helpful way, of course), and we hope our children and grandchildren will appreciate this book. Deborah, who is pursuing graduate studies in ethnomusicology at Kent State University, contributed the chapter on Amish music. Virginia typed much of the manuscript and edited and proof-read the final copy, "leaving no stone unturned" in getting the text to say exactly what we wanted. In the sense of getting this book to market, this has truly been a group project. We hope you will like the book and will develop some thought-provoking insights about a very special people as you read. These are the Amish people of North America.

Bruce K. Friesen
John W. Friesen
August, 1996

References

Hostetler, John A. (1993). *Amish Society.* fourth edition. Baltimore, MD: The Johns Hopkins University Press.

Nolt, Stephen M. (1992). *A History of the Amish.* Intercourse, PA: Good Books.

Peter, Karl A. (1987). *The Dynamics of Hutterite Society: An Analytic Approach.* Edmonton, AB: University of Alberta Press.

The Parameters of Cultural Pluralism

Strangely enough, the very freedom we seek cannot be attained until we chain some of our exaggerated individuality.

—*Gerald Emmett Carter, Archbishop of Toronto.*

The alternative of cultural pluralism as a societal format is of fairly recent derivation in the United States even though the country may be described as a nation of immigrants. Between 1820 and 1970, for example, more than 45 million immigrants, mostly from European nations, took up residence in the United States (Bennett, 1990). Initially the plan was to assimilate all newcomers into the American way of life, and to help them, by force if necessary, to become part of the great melting-pot. The official view of both government bureaucrats and educators regarding immigrants nearly a century ago was to ". . . break up their groups and settlements, to assimilate or amalgamate these people as part of the American race, and to implant in their children, so far as can be done, the Anglo-Saxon conception of righteousness, law, order, and popular government . . ." (Cubberly, 1909).

Defining Cultural Pluralism

In its most academic form, cultural pluralism (sometimes also known as multiculturalism) relies on the process of compromise characterized by mutual appreciation and respect between two or more ethnic groups (Friesen, 1993). It implies a commitment to the development of all cultural groups, and even hints at governmental assistance in overcoming the cultural barriers which would impede their full participation in society. In effect, cultural pluralism has been delineated as a new social policy (Fleras and Elliott, 1992). As an expression of a social goal, it suggests respect for and support of the heritages and cultures of the various ethnocultural groups within a given society, with the end-in-view of providing equity for all citizens.

Figure 1-1. Parking on a Market day.

The dilemma of trying to accommodate cultural differences while at the same time assure equal treatment for all is the pivotal paradox of cultural pluralism. As Pai (1990) has stated:

> The central problem of cultural pluralism is how minority groups can maintain enough separation from the dominant cultures to perpetuate and develop their own ethnic traditions without, at the same time, interfering with the execution of their responsibilities to the society of which they are members (16–17).

Sadly, it is often the adoption of generalized cultural values, goals and structures which ignore whole sectors of society that have enabled countries like the United States and Canada to forge ahead economically. Some will argue that this factor has permitted the development of the very institutional advances that provide wealth and which are criticized today for their contributions towards creating an economically stratified society. Max Weber, the classical German sociologist postulated that a generalized national set of values enabled profit-making and the accumulation of capital, which then also became dominant social goals. The great innovation of Protestantism, when it appeared in 16th century Europe, was to help develop a way of culturally seeing the world in which economic and religious attainment did not contradict each other. One could be a successful capitalist without feeling religiously negligent (Russell, 1994). Multiculturalism draws a halt to that development by positing that there might be another way to accomplish this goal without forcing a cultural strait-jacket on all citizens.

It was early in the 20th century that the concept of cultural pluralism first received any serious measure of national attention. Philosopher, Horace Meyer Kallin (1882–1974), came to America from Poland around the turn of the century and argued strongly against the deliberate assimilation of immigrants, claiming instead that they be allowed to retain their cultural heritages even though becoming patriotic American citizens (Kallin, 1924; Bennett, 1990). In similar fashion, Jane Addams, who was actively engaged in the settlement of immigrants working at Hull House in Chicago, protested against the treatment of immigrants in sweatshops and worked to get factory laws changed to protect them (Miller-Lachmann and Taylor, 1995). It was not until the protest movements of the 1960s, that is civil rights, women's liberation, Black power, and Vietnam War protests, however, that these ideas were afforded much attention (Gay, 1983). Gradually the policy evolved, at least in theoretical form, that cultural minorities should be encouraged to be proud of their ethnic heritage instead of being ashamed of their differences (Tiedt and Tiedt, 1995). Along with this development was the encouraged shift to a new expectation of public tolerance and acceptance of unique cultural lifestyles. Cultural pluralism is even currently touted as a healthy national composition, but not necessarily to the extent of heightening ethnic group identity to the point of causing fragmentation or intergroup antagonism as is sometimes charged. According to some observers, multiculturalism is widely viewed as a developing national policy (Bennett, 1990).

The Complications of Cultural Pluralism

There are numerous barriers to fulfilling the commitment to multiculturalism in America, including a fuzzy definition, lack of financial resources and the fact that supportive studies are conducted by "academic ethnocentrics" (scholars who tend to take themselves too seriously), who end up promoting a form of academic ghettoization (Grant and Millar, 1992). In light of the relatively recent origins of multiculturalism it is well to keep in mind that social movements come and go even if at any given time they are viewed as more or less permanent fixtures. House (1992) suggests that nationalism, for example, is a recent player (late 18th century) on the international scene, but at the height of its intensity it drives people to the point that they become willing to die for their nation and ethnic community. Apparently, nationalism was generated in part from shared print languages. When cheap newsprint became available, many speakers of the vernacular also became readers for the first time. People began imagining themselves as part of communities which stretched beyond themselves and their immediate villages, even across time. House contends that language is the major instrument of nationalism, and it is primarily the school that is used to teach the local nationalistic vernacular. He admits that nationalism may be economically inspired, but points out (citing Hobsbawm, 1990), that some scholars see it as a transitory phase of capitalism which is bound to dissolve as nations become economically obsolete units and are drawn into larger economic entities (Anderson, 1983; Hobsbawm, 1990; House, 1992).

A second wave of nationalism flourished in America during 1820–1920, when one could witness deliberate attempts to prevent popular nationalist movements overseas by utilizing the apparatus of state cultural and educational institutions to promote loyalty to the mother country. Ironically, similar tactics are employed by pluralist exponents today. This has sometimes motivated a "reverse multiculturalism" in that immigrants to North America have often returned home, disillusioned with the atmosphere of an allegedly tolerant society. For example, Beaujot (1991) estimates that 30 percent of the immigrants who arrived in Canada between 1951–1970 and 20 percent of those who arrived between 1971–1980 had returned home by 1986. As a further indicator, 43 percent of the immigrants who arrived between 1978 and 1982, and 28 percent of the 1967–1977 arrivals had not taken out Canadian citizenship by 1986 (Jansen and Richmond, 1990).

The challenge of formulating a functional mix of multiculturalism with the democratic process often produces tensions with national implications. As Gordon (1964) has pointed out, when pluralism *is* encouraged, questions quickly arise pertaining to the extent to which separatism can be practiced without risk to the general national welfare. If culturally divergent groups are awarded the right to preserve the basic elements of their lifestyle, at what point does this arrangement run the risk of interfering with the rights of others? To what extent does the existence and practice of cultural separateness contribute towards the welfare of the nation as a whole? In Gordon's words:

> The major problem, then, is to keep ethnic separation in communal life from being so pronounced in itself that it threatens ethnic harmony, good group relations, and the spirit of good will which a democratic pluralistic society requires, and to keep it from spilling over into the civic arena of secondary education to impinge on housing, jobs, politics, education, and other areas of functional activity where universalistic criteria of judgment and assignment are necessary and where the operation of ethnic considerations can only be disruptive and even disastrous. The attainment of this objective calls for good sense and reasonableness on the part of the average American citizen . . . (Gordon, 1964, 264).

Gordon's phrase, "good sense and reasonableness" offers the clue to appreciating the complexity of cultural pluralism as an applied goal. It is difficult to conceive of a situation where pluralism is void of educational, civic and political ramifications because these represent the very arenas in which applications are undertaken. Moreover, ethnicity *does* affect schooling, class membership and earnings, although to understand this phenomenon fully, it is necessary to also take into account other sources of inequality (Li, 1988, 125). Opponents of cultural pluralism have aptly pointed out that a truly multicultural and multiracial society is hard to govern because of the difficulties in forming and maintaining functional political coalitions. Tensions among groups may erupt because of competition for housing, jobs or other resources. The debates over the outcome, content and processes of schooling will similarly be a major concern (Henry, 1990).

A democratic society is by definition committed to discussion and debate as the various issues propelled by freedom of speech are deliberated. At the core of such discussions is a potential analysis of the nature of democracy itself, which in the case of a pluralist society, is similarly open to debate. The dominant group will logistically set the limits of acceptable democratic behaviour, and define what is normative behaviour. Still, there are numerous examples to indicate that the parameters of defined "normative" behaviour are easily violated. For example: refusal of Amish people to send their children to public schools, Mormon practice of polygamy, Jehovah Witnesses refusing to salute the flag, Vietnamese boys not taking orders from female teachers, Blacks starting Afrocentric schools, and Hindu men burning brides because of insufficient dowries (House, 1992). A similar situation prevails in Canada. For example,

- over the past half century we have seen government restrictions on Hutterite land purchases because of citizens' objections to their communal way of life;
- removal of Japanese Canadians from their homes and confiscation of their goods and businesses during World War II, solely on the grounds of their allegedly undesirable visible (racial) appearance;
- government refusal to honor First Nations' land claims on grounds that they involve heavily-populated urban areas;
- refusal of the Québécois government to allow the children of non-Anglophone immigrants to be taught in English in provincial schools;
- refusal of the Alberta Government to allow French to be spoken in the legislature even though French is an official national language; and,
- refusal of the Canadian government to apologize or recognize any legal obligations to the Ukrainian people who were incarcerated during the Second World War because of their alleged suspicious loyalties.

Recently there have been public objections to the new policy that members of the Sikh faith can wear traditional head-gear while serving with the Royal Canadian Mounted Police. This stance may be questioned on two grounds; first, it is recognized that the RCMP uniform was originally a gift from Britain, and second, the force has already changed its uniform in four major ways since its inception in 1874. Somehow, objectors claimed that by granting Sikhs this right the action was somehow violating a revered *Canadian* tradition (Berger, 1982).

House (1992) points out that there are definite differences in the way Canada and the U.S.A. perceive multiculturalism. He suggests that Americans are brash nationalists, while Canadians tend to be "closet nationalists". Differences between USA and Canadian approaches to multiculturalism are symbolized by the melting-pot and mosaic metaphors (137). A Canadian sociologist, John Porter, defined Canadians (in contrast to the Americans), as conservative, authoritarian and more oriented to tradition, hierarchy, and elitism in the sense of showing deference to those in high status, and united in defense of these values against the egalitarianism and aggressiveness of American culture (Porter, 1987). As House notes:

Both societies [USA and Canada] experienced immense migration from 1850 to 1914 and again since World War II. In the most recent decade, 1980 to 1990, for example, the Hispanic population of the United States increased by 7.7 millions, a 56 percent increase. Twenty-five percent of the U.S. population is now minority, up from 20 percent in 1980, the largest population change this century (Barringer, 1991). New immigrants then and now have been greeted with hostility manifested in nativist movements (House, 1992, 137).

Those who worship unquestioningly at the shrine of democracy are sometimes shocked to discover that its format can be subject to change without inflicting permanent damage. Undoubtedly the changing ethnic composition of the U.S.A. has political, philosophical and pedagogical ramifications as the various shifting segments of society impinge their opinions upon the democratic process, possibly even redefining its traditionally-revered essence. Gay (1992) suggests that world developments are causing some Americans, at least, to reconsider their country's traditional role of international dominance and unquestionable leadership in world affairs. In an attempt to summarize the feelings of the American people on the topic, then USA presidential candidate, Bill Clinton, accused President Bush of being too concerned about international affairs and neglecting the needs of the American people. The fast-changing international scene is hard to keep up with, let alone adjust to, even from a democratic perspective. Japan's economic and technological might has severely threatened America's influence in the world marketplace, and the increasing rate and magnitude of foreign investments in North America generally has raised doubts about the validity of a North American continentalism. There are other happenings such as the crumbling of the communistic bloc in Eastern Europe, the reunification of Germany, escalations of tensions in the Middle East and the relaxation of the South African government on apartheid that similarly reflect the fast-changing direction of today's world. The involvement of the United States in these situations is extensive and has expanded the contextual parameters of multiculturalism to global dimensions. The resultant situation is not one for which the traditional American "quick-fix" orientation will necessarily produce a ready solution (Gay, 1992).

Liberal Democracy

The central focus of a liberal democracy, such as that of Canada or the USA is a respect for individual equality and the economic marketplace. A further interpretation promulgated by liberal multiculturalists is that the members of the body politick will have respect for differing cultural identities *and* for the common bond that makes them a society. The difficulty that emerges from the discussion is that *group rights* are not an entity in the United Nations context because in delineating its parameters of recognized rights that body foresaw that minority or group claims could be dangerously threatening to the national stability of some member nation-states. Against that context, ethnocultural communities or minority groups have no *international* grounds for claiming collective recognition. Individuals *do* have rights, however, and these are supposed to be protected by national and international law, and as such, furnish the individual with the freedom to choose to retain or not to retain cultural connections or identity. That freedom is a fragile commodity, however, in a world where human rights are beset by ideology and orthodoxy, where diversity is rejected and dissent is stifled (Berger, 1982).

All of this places the urgency of multicultural policy and practice on extremely precarious grounds and raises doubts about the efficacy of the pluralist principle. Glazer (1988), for example, construes ethnic membership as an individual, private, and voluntary matter, like belonging to a club or choosing one's associates or deciding which college to attend. He treats ethnicity as a matter of personal choice and argues against *any* measure of group rights, stressing instead that only *individuals have rights*, not groups. To illustrate, House (1992) emphasizes that even Aboriginal rights in America are treated as *gifts* which can be revoked; they are not rights. He suggests that only when a minority culture is actually threatened are special rights justified. Even then, no cultural custom or practice should be permitted if it violates the individual rights guaranteed by the nation even if it is argued by the minority in question that the practice is essential to the maintenance of their culture.

A similar situation prevails in Canada where ethnicity has been entrenched in law and is allegedly protected by the Federal Charter of Rights and Freedoms (Friesen, 1992). In effect the Charter has made little difference, and even its goal of encouraging national unity has been "fragile and often threatened by intolerance" (Trudeau, 1990, 366). In essence, the implementation of the spirit and intent of the Charter is dependent upon the "will and spirit of the people" (Ray, 1985, 10). For example, the Charter does not have the authority to override existing laws that violate human rights. This is because parts of the Charter are interpretive; they do not *confer* rights, but rather allow for a behaviour translation which is supposed to be consistent with "the preservation and enhancement of [the] multicultural heritage of Canada" (Leal, 1983, 25). Thus the Charter is a passive instrument, at best indicative of a long-range social goal or envisaged ideology. It is not meant to be a spur; it is meant to be a brake. It prohibits racial discrimination in law, but it cannot require governments or citizens to promote racial (or cultural) equality (Matas, 1991).

Against this background it would seem logical to conclude that a genuine North American culturally-plural society is still a long way off. In the meantime the sloganizing about multiculturalism will no doubt continue, hopefully, with the eventual end that a closer correlation will emerge between official policy and practice. Undoubtedly world events and the changing national cultural composition will augur strongly as related factors in the transition.

Practical Concerns

The above observation raises serious questions about the potential importance of multiculturalism as a reachable societal objective. One of the institutions most likely to be affected is the school, particularly in the case of such traditionally-oriented groups as the Amish. Schooling is doubly important in our society because there is a relative lack of alternative models of influence. Thus our focus is upon the school as a context for the acquisition and confirmation of ethnic and racial beliefs of visible and non-visible minorities. However, before we can discuss the specifics of the educational system, we must place the issue in a larger context.

In spite of the initiatives identified above, we have not been able to implement the multicultural policies that imply the equality of all citizens. Often these policies are misunderstood by developers and implementers alike. Some see the policies as forms of cultural preservation while others see them as means of addressing social injustice. Still others view them as guaranteeing "special rights" for certain minorities and, therefore, a threat to national unity.

Two decades ago, when policy makers first initiated formal policies of multiculturalism they were not precise in their objectives and the implementers did not firmly grasp the fundamental principles enunciated in these policies. In the end, the policies have never been successfully communicated as something relevant to all citizens. By the 1980s, these policies began to focus on race relations and the development of strategies related to this area. This new approach came about as a kind of demographic revolution was taking place with large numbers of immigrants arriving from Asia, Africa, the Middle East and Latin America, and declining numbers from traditional European sources. The American Census Bureau indicated massive increases in the populations of Asians and Pacific Islanders, Hispanics, Blacks and Native Americans during the 1980s. As a result of immigration, and the high fertility and varying morality codes of other groups, the proportion of whites in the overall population has declined to 71 percent, while Blacks comprise about 12 percent, Hispanics about 9 percent and Asians just under 3 percent (Fleras and Elliott, 1992). The largest Asian-American groups live primarily on the west coast, with pockets in the Midwest and New York. Mexican-Americans and Amerindian populations are primarily in the southwest, Puerto Ricans in the northeast, and Cubans in the mid-Atlantic and south Atlantic states. Blacks remain concentrated in the south. By contrast, only about 3 percent of Americans can lay claim to being truly "native" Americans, that is, Amerindians, Eskimos (Inuit), Aleutian Islanders and Hawaiians (Grant, 1995). Pretty well all of these groups live in urban areas. Estimates are that "by the year 2000 over a third of students nation-wide will be from an ethnic minority" (Siccone, 1995, xi).

Cultural preservation has not a primary concern to these new immigrants. By contrast it has always been of serious concern to the already-established third and fourth generation of ethnocultural groups. The "rediscovery" of ethnicity among the established groups has dictated that government originate multicultural policies to address these cultural and heritage issues among well-established citizens. This resulted in a multicultural approach that was bifurcated in its thrust. Different interest groups emerged who questioned the direction of the policy. As a result the policy and its implementation came under scrutiny and criticism from many quarters. Many resident immigrants abandoned their "house guest" mentality and attempted to enter the institutional life of mainstream society. They became aware of how these institutions operated and they now wanted "in". No longer content to be spectators, they insisted on becoming active participants in society. Some were even ready to renounce their ancestral cultures in favor of the behaviour and values of the Anglo-Saxon core group (Gollnick and Chinn, 1986). In short, there has been a transformation in the self-perception and actions of these communities. In the absence of clear-cut goals and objectives, social cleavages have multiplied and amplified. Multiculturalism is perceived as fostering ethnic exclusivity by the larger dominant society. It is gradually being viewed as under obligation to accommodate the needs and wishes of ethnocultural communities as well as mainstream citizens.

Educational Concerns

The school of thought promoting multiculturalism within an educational context reveals several forms of implementation that have been advocated. First, there are those proponents who articulate a discourse of cultural understanding. This approach is inscribed in university-offered human relations programs which place a premium on "improving communication" among various ethnic groups. The fundamental stance of this approach is that of cultural relativism. Cultural relativism is translated in curriculum guides for ethnic studies in terms of a discourse of reciprocity and consensus; we are different, but we are all the same.

A second school of thought emphasizes cultural competence, that is, students need to be educated to appreciate and learn how to function effectively in varying cultural contexts. Underpinning this approach to education is the fundamental assumption that the theme of cultural pluralism should have a central place in the curriculum of the schools. This concept of social institutions as sites for the confluence of a plurality of ethnic interests was formulated in the 1960s. The proponents of this approach argue that multicultural education is education which values cultural pluralism. They reject the view that schools should merely *tolerate* cultural pluralism, but instead, *affirm* that schools should be oriented towards the cultural enrichment of all students through programs rooted in the preservation and extension of cultural alternatives. Educators who promote the idea of cultural competence reform argue for various forms of bilingual and ethnic studies programs based on pluralist values that would help to build bridges between different ethnic communities (Sleeter and Grant, 1988). These programs aim at preserving cultural diversity. It is expected that students from the dominant group will acquire knowledge of and gain familiarity with the languages and cultures of communities other than their own. It is felt that such cross-cultural interaction will contribute to reduced ethnic and racial antagonism between majority and minority students.

A third model goes further than the two above and is referred to as the "cultural emancipation model". It suggests that an anti-racist multicultural curriculum can boost both the school success and economic futures of minority youth. This reform-oriented curriculum is to include knowledge about minority history and cultural achievements, and thereby help reduce the dissonance and alienation from academic success that centrally characterize minority experiences in school. Such a reformed school curriculum is expected to enhance minority opportunities for academic success and assure better futures in the labor market.

All of the approaches noted above attach an enormous significance to the role of attitudes in the reproduction and transformation of racism. As such these models focus almost exclusively on the reversal of values, attitudes and human nature of social actors in understanding individuals. In each of these models, the school for example, is conceptualized as a site of power or contestation in which differential resources and capacities determine the manoeuvrability of competing racial groups and the possibility and pace of change. These approaches fail to take into account the differential structure opportunities that help to define race. Moreover, these theoretical models tend to emphasize the addition of new content about minority history and culture to the curriculum and focus on the individual as the unit of analysis. The multicultural strategy of adding diversity to the dominant school curriculum serve, paradoxically, to legitimize the dominance of western culture in educational arrangements. A critical multiculturalism should be more reflexive with respect to the relationship between different social groups and the relationship of national developments to the rest of the world. In short, a more structuralist conceptualization of how education operates needs to be taken into account. An effective form of multiculturalism would offer hope to those who have been isolated from the arteries of educational progress.

Useful Models

Gibson's (1976) schematic is helpful in elaborating the historical approaches to the problem of fair delivery of multicultural programs, and identifies four models originated by educators in the beginning stages of the development of multicultural education. These included (i) education of the culturally different; (ii) education about cultural differences; (iii) education for cultural pluralism; and (iv) bicultural education. The first approach, education of the culturally different is clearly assimilative in intent and is aimed at bringing the educational levels of schooling in minority group communities "up to par" with the rest of society. In this approach, all adjustments are to be made by minority members since it is assumed that their educational status is somehow lacking in comparison with that of the dominant monoculture.

The second approach, education *about* cultural differences, is targeted at the promotion of cultural understanding by teaching an appreciation for the ethnic and cultural diversity within the nation's schools. Gamlin, Berndorff, Mitsopulos, and Demetriou (1994) suggest that this phase focuses on introducing "song and dance" activities as a minor aspect of the total curricular approach—an approach which emphasizes specific ethnic-cultural perspectives. Critics have pointed out that the school has traditionally failed in this function largely because the curriculum is assimilative in intent and based on premises inherent in a white Anglo-Saxon Protestant orientation (Henley and Young, 1981). Those located at the bottom of the resultant stratificational scale have undoubtedly failed to embrace the virtues of the protestant ethic, namely,the importance of hard work and thrift as key social values (Elliott and Fleras, 1992).

The third approach fares little better with the critics since the school is hardly capable of educating for cultural pluralism with any far-reaching consequences. It would take more influence than schooling is capable of to achieve any degree of success in a domain that affects all of the basic structures of society including business, politics, religion, economics, and the like. Implicit in this approach is the belief that the state has the responsibility of helping all ethnic groups to preserve their heritage languages and cultures. Schools employing this approach also attempt to enhance harmonious relations among their various ethnocultural sectors by means of curriculum emphases, exchange visits and collaboration.

Gibson's final approach to multicultural education is called "biculturalism," and implies that the learner be educated to be able to function effectively within two different cultural contexts—that of dominant society and that within their own ethnocultural communities. In the early 1980s, multicultural education began to consider broader issues such as equity, stressing not only equity of opportunity, but equity of outcomes (Gamlin, et al., 1994). This approach focussed on intercultural understanding, including human relations, cultural sharing and human rights. This final stage (bi/multicultural education), is referred to as the "transcultural" option by which the teacher encourages members of various ethnic groups to go beyond the borders of their group and appreciate or take on elements of other ethnic communities. Here there is a fusion of cultures to actively create a new culture (Caccia, 1984; Robin, 1989).

It is questionable that any individual can achieve the competencies required to function equally well in two different societies, and, should this objective be fulfilled, it may produce a kind of cultural schizophrenia or marginality indicative of living in two different worlds but being truly at home in neither (Friesen, 1983). At best the individual may formulate a functional framework of values which represent one or the other of the two cultural alternatives or develop a personally-concocted unique admixture. In rare cases the development of an attitude of tolerance towards and an understanding of other cultural systems may evolve.

A second schematic by Ouellet (1992) outlining four options for multicultural teaching is targeted at dealing with the problems of conflicting ideologies and relativism which are composite in a culturally-plural society. Assimilationists quickly object to any plan which they fear may fragment the system. They resent any action on the part of state officials to promote other than a "systems" approach to education. Cultural pluralists, on the other hand, opt for a more flexible and perhaps less efficient approach that would recognize and foster more divergent lifestyles. The diversity of envisaged goals can possibly be reduced to four options:

   (i)   the monocultural option, in which the state tries to socialize all citizens to an appreciation of the "national culture";
   (ii) the multicultural option, in which the state has the responsibility to help all ethnic groups to preserve their language and heritage;
   (iii) the intercultural option, in which the state is to enhance harmonious relations among its various ethnocultural sectors by means of exchange and collaboration; and
   (iv) the transcultural option, in which the state must encourage the members of the various ethnic groups to go beyond the borders of their group and face with creativity and dynamism the new challenges raised by the acceleration of change in the world economy.

The availability of models not withstanding, lack of appropriate technique, lack of teacher skills and confusion as to which goal is desired have all resulted in failing policies and practices. Until recently, educators have taken the position that the dominant system is superior to all others, but to be blunt, the underlying assumption implies that the western way is not to be questioned. In some cases, when multicultural policies *have* been introduced in schools, for many people this has precipitated a crisis. The issue of multicultural education has been and remains an issue which provokes passion that is rare for most other educational issues. The introduction of English-as-a-second-language programs have stirred up nationalist feelings and reactions from right-wing groups and media who fear that they are being swamped by "alien cultures".

Where students fail because of poor policies or programs, or confused goals, the failure is attributed to the lack of educational motivation, if not to the cultural particularities of students. The conservative onslaught on multicultural curricula in educational institutions, under the rubric of "political correctness" has set a new agenda. Small and modest challenges to the Anglo-elite culture have been met by a reaction that only confirms its dominance.

Perhaps multiculturalism, like nationalism and other such themes, has had its day, even before it culminates in a full fruition. In the meantime as dedicated educators continue to attempt to transform an underlying assimilative stance towards a culturally pluralist format they might do well not to neglect the other factors that distinguish human diversity, that is, other distinctions or uniquenesses which weigh heavily in the campaign to define the human species more sharply in an effort to better achieve equality for all. These include the physical aspect (including biological, racial or hereditary), and the political, social, psychological and religious, to say nothing of individual differences in perception. This in no way diminishes the significance of noting cultural differences, although each categorical difference is worthy of separate emphasis.

The Challenge

Over the past two decades, conservatives have had a good deal of success in redefining what education is for and in shifting the ideological texture of society profoundly to the right (Apple, 1988). This is particularly true where human rights are discussed. There is a recurrent conflict between property rights and individual rights that has been central in our culture. Property rights have vested in individuals the power to enter into social relationships based on the nature and extent of property. On the other hand, individual rights vest in persons the power to enter into these relationships on the basis of simple membership in the social collectivity (Gintis, 1980). Dominant group members have generally favored property rights as the basis for entering into social relationships, while minority groups have fought for person rights. For many years the right to vote was contingent upon having personal property of minimum value. The depressed economy of today has led many people to argue that person rights should be rescinded because they were too expensive to maintain. In short, gains made by minority groups in the past should be given up in order to deal with financial reality. For example, special education programs currently operating for the benefit of specific ethnocultural groups should be dismantled.

The new conservativism has embarked on the concentrated task of convincing the public that the notion of person rights is not an acceptable way of entering into the social mainstream. At the most generalized level, the argument is that the state should not be a major actor in trying to overcome the disadvantages of minorities, that individual disadvantage is not the result of being a member of an oppressed minority or having other historical disadvantage, but rather the simple choice of an individual *not* to overcome their personal disadvantages. Failure is no longer a product of the system, but rather a personal defect. According to this new conservativism, individuals are ". . . unequal, autonomous, moral agents who are responsible for the consequences that befall them" (Ungerleider, 1993, 19).

The results of this new ideology have led to a deep imbrication of traditional, canonical school knowledge that has legitimized authority and inequality in society. Conservative politicians and business leaders have responded vigorously to the multicultural challenge and within the past few years there has been a virtual reaffirmation of Eurocentric and western culture in debates over the school curriculum and educational reform (Ravitch, 1990; Schlesinger, 1991). The expression of this new conservativism has taken many different forms.

Some individuals acknowledge a useful role for multiculturalism only if it means accurately representing the historical contributions of various ethnic groups to the building of societal institutions, for example, First Nations, Blacks, and women, who have hitherto been understood only from the standpoint of the dominant British, male intellectual establishment. Many critics will argue that the promotion of multiculturalism is not only socially divisive but also represents bad history in that it dishonors the quest for objective truth in scholarship. It deliberately distorts to serve the vested political interests of social activists and bureaucrats and professionals in the public sphere. It is romanticized in that it is manipulated to provide therapeutic relief and emotional comfort to minorities even though they do not seem to want it. According to Schlesinger (1991), they want assimilation and integration.

The debate about multiethnic or multicultural education and the attendant problems has produced a new perspective—an antiracist perspective. Antiracist educators are not content with the status quo of multicultural education. They believe that traditional kinds of multicultural education do not necessarily affect the cognitive domain (Friesen, 1995). They reject multicultural education on the basis that its programs allegedly offer only superficial information about cultural diversity and obscure the fundamental facts of racial, white hegemony in all domains of society, including schooling. They advocate, without apology, deliberate indoctrinative approaches that will promote intercultural and multicultural awareness and appreciation. The contemporary form of multicultural education is rejected because it falsely suggests equality where there is none.

Multicultural education has had little impact in developing a pluralistic society. Nor has it diminished the ethnic inequality. The question as to how education can contribute to the development of social solidarity lies unanswered. An effective multicultural policy must therefore be developed to address not only mainstream concerns with regard to national unity, but it must deal with issues such as racism and prejudice (Gamlin, et al., 1994). As Paquet (1991) points out, polyethnicity has become a North American reality with millions of citizens representing a myriad of backgrounds and value systems. Accompanying the growth of these populations has been an increased knowledge base of culturally diverse children. An improved knowledge of culturally different people has enlightened people to a point where it is not necessary to be suspicious, or to fail to understand others' customs and traditions, or to question their worth as human beings (Baruth and Manning, 1992). Any policy, if it is to be successful, must reflect that diversity, and avoid becoming a uniform nation-building public philosophy.

The Amish Way

Although resident in North America since the early 18th century, the Amish have always tried to ignore the ongoings in dominant society except where they were forced to involve themselves by economic necessity. Seeking to practice their religious convictions faithfully, they have inadvertently also tested the parameters of cultural pluralism in America. In fact, it was their wish to live their faith in an "unmolested and undisturbed" manner that

Figure 1-2. Old-fashioned machinery—still in use.

prompted them to leave Europe and migrate to America in the early part of the 18th century. Subsequent clashes with the government have pertained mainly with regard to military conscription and schooling, particularly in the early decades of this century.

A central premise of Amish life is separation of church and state. They perceive a gulf between their church and the world which has been imprinted in their consciousness by decades of persecution (Kraybill, 1993). Over the past three centuries they have also developed a unique, traditional lifestyle which in many ways contradicts that of dominant society. It remains immersed in a past lifestyle which all Americans once knew. Culturally and socially, they are essentially a separate people, even though they have adopted very limited forms of modern technology. The Amish pay taxes, as other citizens do, and bear the additional cost of operating private alternative schools which were declared within the law by USA Supreme Court action in May, 1972 (Keim, 1975).

Riesman (1950) differentiated American society in terms of tradition-directed individuals and groups who cling to their rigid old ways with reference to such phrases as "submission to the will of God" (Hostetler, 1980, 182), and other-directed individuals and groups who manifest highly flexible personality patterns involving openness to change, often through imitating the behaviour of others. Riesman accused most Americans of being so other-directed that their performances could differ markedly from those which they evidenced in church, at home or at a party. Such a shifting personality would mark a person as untrustworthy in a traditional society, but flexible enough to do well in dominant society (Macionis, 1989). The difficulty for the tradition-directed Amish, is that the control of society is in the hands of other-directed individuals who have the power to delineate the parameters of any forms of social deviancy. Through the years they have lived in North America the Amish have managed to clear quite some hurdles in gaining a measured form of approval to live their particular lifestyle. Their experience marks one of the most profound examples of celebrating extraordinary group (cultural) rights in America.

References

Anderson, B. (1983). *Imagined Communities: Reflections on the Origin and Spread of Nationalism.* London: Verso.

Apple, M. W. (1988). *Teachers and Texts: A Political Economy of Class and Gender Relations.* New York: Routledge.

Barringer, F. (1991). Census shows profound change in racial makeup of the nation, *New York Times,* A1, A12.

Baruth, Leroy and M. Lee Manning. (1992). *Multicultural Education of Children and Adolescents.* Needham Heights, MA: Allyn and Bacon.

Beaujot, R. (1991). *Population Change in Canada.* Toronto, ON: McClelland and Stewart.

Bennett, Christine I. (1990). *Comprehensive Multicultural Education: Theory and Practice.* second edition. Boston: Allyn and Bacon.

Berger, Thomas R. (1982). *Fragile Freedoms: Human Rights and Dissent in Canada.* Toronto, ON: Irwin.

Caccia, F. (1984). L'ethnicité Comme Post-modernité. *Vice Versa.* 2:1, 12–13, 223.

Cubberly, E. (1909). *Changing Conceptions of Education.* Boston: Houghton- Mifflin.

Elliott, Jean Leonard and Augie Fleras. (1992). *Unequal Relations: An Introduction to Race and Ethnic Dynamics in Canada:* Scarborough, ON: Prentice-Hall.

Fleras, Augie and Jean Leonard Elliott. (1992). *Multiculturalism in Canada: The Challenge of Diversity.* Scarborough, ON: Nelson Canada

Friesen, John W. (1983). *Schools With A Purpose.* Calgary, AB: Detselig Enterprises.

Friesen, John W. (1992). *Multiculturalism in Canada: Hope or Hoax?* Edmonton, AB: Alberta Teachers' Association.

Friesen , John W. (1993). *When Cultures Clash: Case Studies in Multiculturalism.* second edition. Calgary: Detselig Enterprises.

Friesen, John W. (1995). Multicultural Education as a Component of Formal Socialization. *Readings in Child Development.* Katherine Covell, ed. Toronto, ON: Nelson Canada, 172–184.

Gamlin, P., D. Berndorff, A. Mitsopulos and K. Demetriou. (1994). Multicultural Education in Canada from a Global Perspective. *Ethnicity and Culture in Canada: The Research Landscape.* J. Berry and J. Laponce, eds. Toronto, ON: University of Toronto Press, 112–130.

Gay, Geneva. (1983). Multiethnic Education: Historical Development and Future Prospects, *Phi Delta Kappan,* 64: April, 560–561.

Gay, Geneva. (1992). Multicultural Education in the United States, *Beyond Multicultural Education: International Perspectives.* Kogila A. Moodley, ed. Calgary, AB: Detselig Enterprises, 41–66.

Gibson, Margaret. (1976). Approaches to Multicultural Education in the U.S.: Some Concepts and Assumptions, *Anthropology and Education Quarterly,* 7:4, 7–18.

Gintis, H. (1980). Communication and Politics. *Socialist Review.* March–June, 189–232.

Glazer, N. (1988). The Affirmative Action Stalemate. *The Public Interest,* 90: 99–114.

Gollnick, Donna M. and Philip C. Chinn. (1986). *Multicultural Education in a Pluralistic Society.* Columbus, OH: Charles E. Merrill Publishing Company.

Gordon, Milton M. (1964). *Assimilation in American Life: The Role of Race, Religion and National Origins.* New York: Oxford University Press.

Grabb, Edward G. (1990). *Theories of Social Inequality: Classical and Contemporary Perspectives.* second edition. Toronto, ON: Holt, Rinehart and Winston.

Grant, Carl A., ed. (1995). *Educating for Diversity: An Anthology of Multicultural Voices.* Boston: Allyn and Bacon.

Grant, Carl A. and Susan Millar. (1992). Research and Multicultural Education: Barriers, Needs and Boundaries, *Beyond Multicultural Education: International Perspectives.* Kogila A. Moodley, ed. Calgary, AB: Detselig Enterprises, 201–214.

Havighurst, Robert J. and Bernice L. Neugarten. *Society and Education.* fourth edition. Boston: Allyn and Bacon.

Henley, Richard and Jonathan Young. (1981). Multicultural Education: Contemporary Variations on a Historical Theme, *The History and Social Science Teacher,* 17:1, Fall, 7–16.

Henry III, W.A. (1990). Beyond the Melting Pot, *Time,* 135: 28–31.

Hobsbawm, E. J. (1990). *Nations and Nationalism Since 1780.* Cambridge, MA: Cambridge University Press.

Hostetler, John A. (1980). *Amish Society.* third edition. Baltimore, MD: The Johns Hopkins University Press.

House, Ernest R. (1992). Multicultural Evaluation in Canada and the United States, *The Canadian Journal of Program Evaluation,* 7:1, 133–156.

Jansen, C. and A. Richmond. (1990). *Immigrant Settlement and Integration in Canada.* Toronto: Unpublished Paper.

Kallen, Evelyn. (1989). *Label Me Human: Minority Rights of Stigmatized Canadians.* Toronto, ON: University of Toronto Press.

Kallin, Horace Meyer. (1924). *Culture and Democracy in the United States.* New York: Boni and Liveright.

Keim, Albert N. (1975). A Chronology of Amish Court Cases. *Compulsory Education and the Amish: The Right Not to be Modern.* Albert N. Keim, ed. Boston: Beacon Press. 93–96.

Kraybill, Donald B. (1993). Negotiating with Caesar. *The Amish and the State.* Donald B. Kraybill, ed. Baltimore, MD: The Johns Hopkins University Press, 3–22.

Leal, H. A. (1983). Multiculturalism and the Charter of Rights and Freedoms, *Multiculturalism,* 8:1, 24–28.

Li, Peter S. (1988). *Ethnic Inequality in a Class Society.* Toronto: Thompson Educational Publishing Co.

Macionis, John. (1989). *Sociology.* second edition. Englewood Cliffs, NJ: Prentice Hall.

Matas, D. (1991). The Charter and Racism, *Currents: Readings in Race Relations,* 7:1, April, 14–15.

Miller-Lachmann, Lyn and Lorraine S. Taylor. (1995). *Schools for All: Educating Children in a Diverse Society.* Albany, NY: Delmar Publishers.

Moodley, Kogila A., ed (1992). *Beyond Multicultural Education: International Perspectives.* Calgary: Detselig Enterprises.

Ouellet, Fernand. (1992). Education in a Pluralistic Society: Proposal for an Enrichment of Teacher Education, *Beyond Multicultural Education: International Perspectives.* Kogila A. Moodley, ed. Calgary, AB: Detselig Enterprises, 281–302.

Pai. Y. (1990). Cultural Pluralism, Democracy and Multiculturalism. *Adult Education in a Multicultural Society.* B. Cassara, ed. New York: Routledge.

Paquet, G. (1991). Political Philosophy of Multiculturalism. *Ethnicity and Culture in Canada: The Research Landscape.* J. Berry, and J. Laponce, eds. Toronto, ON: University of Toronto Press, 60–80.

Porter, John. (1987). *The Measure of Canadian Society: Education, Quality and Opportunity.* Ottawa, ON: Carleton University Press.

Ravitch, D. (1990). Diversity and Democracy: Multicultural Education in America. *American Educator,* 14:1, 16–48.

Ray, Douglas. (1985). Human Rights and Multicultural Perspective in Canada. *Multiculturalism,* 9:1, 10–12.

Riesman, David. (1950). *The Lonely Crowd.* New Haven, CT: Yale University Press.

Ringer, Benjamin B. and Elinor R. Lawless. (1989). *Race, Ethnicity and Society.* London: Routledge.

Robin, R. (1989). la Langre entre l'idéologie et l'utopie. *Vice Versa,* 27:28–32.

Russell, James W. (1994). *After the Fifth Sun: Class and Race in North America.* Englewood Cliffs, NJ: Prentice Hall.

Schlesinger, A.M. (1991). *The Disuniting of America.* Knoxville, TN: Whittle Books.

Siccone, Frank. (1995). *Celebrating Diversity: Building Self-Esteem in Today's Multicultural Classrooms.* Boston: Allyn and Bacon.

Sleeter, C. and C. Grant. (1988). *Making Choices for Multicultural Education: Five Approaches to Race, Class and Culture.* Columbus, OH: Merrill Publishing Company.

Tiedt, Pamela L. and Iris M. Tiedt (1995). *Multicultural Education: a Handbook of Activities, Information and Resources.* fourth edition. Boston: Allyn and Bacon.

Trudeau, Pierre Elliott. (1990). The Values of a Just Society, *Towards a Just Society.* Thomas S. Axworthy and Pierre Elliott Trudeau, eds. Markham, ON: Penguin.

Ungerleider, Charles. (1993). Immigration, Multiculturalism and Citizenship: The Development of the Canadian Social Justice Infrastructure. *Canadian Ethnic Studies,* 24:3, 7–22.

Chapter 2

Perceptions of Amish— in History

Estimations of American Amish population vary widely, but a conservative tally would be that there are nearly 145,000 in North America living in 230 separate communities (Hostetler, 1993). The largest Amish settlement is in Holmes County, Ohio, with a population of 30,000 Amish people, making a total of 43,000 Amish in the State of Ohio. Another 35,000 live in Pennsylvania, most of them in Lancaster County, which is also the home of the largest Mennonite community in both North America and the world, with Winnipeg, Manitoba, playing host to the second largest Mennonite community. Almost half of the American States have Amish living in them.

It is almost impossible to differentiate among the various subgroups of Amish, for example in Wayne County, Ohio, Schreiber (1990) has identified the following groups: Old Order or "House Amish", Beachy Amish, "Conservative" or Church Amish, and "New Amish" Apostolic Christian. The Old Order have further subdivisions such as Swartzentruber, Stutzman and King Amish. The Swartzentruber group, named after an Amish bishop, is clearly one of the most traditional groups. They basically shun any kind of cooperation with any outside group (including other Amish groups), and frequently clash with government authorities over such issues as having to adorn their buggies with SMV (slow-moving vehicle) signs which they think are worldly. They also refuse to haul livestock to market by truck and their farm lanes consist of a set of dirt or mud tracks without added gravel (Zook, 1993).

Amish History

The Amish of North America have a separate history lasting three centuries, but their religious roots go back even further. The Anabaptist background from which they emerged was an integral part of the Protestant Reformation. Considered renegades by the state church, the Anabaptists renounced many mainline doctrines such as infant baptism, confirmation, the sacraments and compulsory church membership, choosing instead to emphasize individualism in faith. This theme greatly contributed towards the constant splintering that has been so much a part of their history ever since.

The Anabaptists

The Protestant Reformation of the 16th century constitutes one of the greatest religious upheavals in the history of the Western world. The long-smoldering fires of discontent and disillusionment with the moral and spiritual corruption in the Medieval Church were fanned into a blazing prairie fire by Martin Luther's posting of his 95 theses on a church door in Wittenburg on October 31, 1517 (Toews, 1975). The thrust of the Reformation split the Christian Church into two major factions in the early part of the 16th century, the movement simultaneously triggered a series of minor factions as well. One of the left-wing groups who opposed all forms of state religion were the Anabaptists, later better known as Mennonites, Hutterites and Amish.

One of the better-known Dutch Anabaptist reformers was a disillusioned former Catholic priest named Menno Simons (1496–1561). Although he claimed he never intended to start a separate church, this is essentially what happened. In 1536 he renounced the Roman Catholic Church and aspired to help develop a new form of "fellowship of believers" emphasizing distinct Anabaptist principles. Soon his followers became known as "Menno People" or "Mennonites". Eventually, a price was on Simons' head and he was forced to go into hiding. His books were banned and his followers were persecuted. So severe was the onslaught against them that on one occasion even Menno's own followers decided to confiscate their leader's writings for their own protection. One individual, Peter von Riesen, who owned some of Menno's writings was twice summoned before the conference of his church and ordered to deliver the whole edition of Menno's writings or he would be excommunicated if he refused (Reimer and Gaeddert, 1956). Still, despite persecution, the Anabaptist movement spread to the German-speaking territory around Switzerland, to south Germany and ultimately to other parts of Europe (Smith, 1957). In Switzerland, the Anabaptist cause was promulgated by a Swiss Reformer, Ulrich Zwingli, who advocated a form of reformed state religion. Zwingli's stand forced a vigorous confrontation between himself and another young Anabaptist reformer named Conrad Grebel, with the latter pulling out of Zwingli's campaign. With this defection, the separate wing of non-Zwinglites thrived (Ruth, 1975).

Historical analysts have sometimes projected that the factionizing tendencies of the Anabaptists were not unique. They point out that there have always been "secessionists" within the Roman Catholic Church, who did not succumb to the sub-Christian worldliness, sacramentalism and clericalism of the church. These included the Montanists of the second century, the Novatians and Catharists of the succeeding generations, the Donatists of the fourth century, the Paulicians of the seventh century, and the Henricians and Petrobrusians of the twelfth century. The most noteworthy of the non-Catholic churches, for the purposes of this historical review, were the Waldensians of the twelfth century, because their beliefs and practices so much resembled those of the Anabaptists (Wenger, 1966). Naturally, most Anabaptist historians reject the theory of "simultaneous dissension" on the grounds that their origins were separate and unique.

Essentially the fundamental beliefs of the Anabaptists may be summarized as follows:

- The Bible is an open book for all and constitutes the sole guide of faith and practice, particularly the New Testament.
- The Church is a voluntary group of believers banded together for the purpose of worship. This implies a rigid separation of church and state and disavows the concept of compulsory state church membership.
- Infant baptism has no place in a voluntary institution because it is the sign of initiation into a universal state church.
- The office of magistrate cannot be filled by the Christian. Government, however, is a Divine institution ordained to protect the righteous and punish the wicked. The Christians must be obedient to their rulers, pray for them, and pay taxes to support the government.
- The Christian cannot take up the sword. Love must be the ruling force in all social relations. It is wrong to kill, either as an individual or by judicial process or miliary force.
- Christians should live secluded from the evil outside world.
- Church discipline is to be secured through the "ban" which is used to exclude the disobedient from the rights of membership. Its practice may appear to be severe but its ultimate objective is to bring the individual to repentance.
- The Lord's Supper is to be regarded merely as a memorial of the death and suffering of Christ, and not as containing the Real Presence.
- It is wrong to take an oath. Christ taught his disciples to give and keep their word without swearing (Harder, 1949, 21–22).

Despite consensus on these very basic doctrines the Anabaptists also held strongly to the notion that the individual is his or her own priest. Thus, in matters of faith, individuals were expected to follow the dictates of their own conscience—unless, of course, those ideas differed from those dictated by the community. One of the first leaders to test this belief was an Austrian hatter named Jacob Hutter, who in 1527 followed Georg Blaurock as leader of the Tyrolean Anabaptist group. Hutter was a man of strong conviction with an aggressive personality and a strict disciplinarian. He advocated that Christians "hold all things in common", based on a passage of scripture in Acts 2:44–45: "All the believers were together and had everything in common. Selling their possessions and goods, they gave to anyone as he had need" (NIV). Hutter taught insistently that a complete break with the past was necessary—followers were urged to leave their homeland and kindred and share with their fellow pilgrims what little possessions they had as a form of resignation or "Gelassenheit" (Hostetler, 1974). By 1530 Hutter's followers had split with the main body of Anabaptist and became known as Hutterites. Today there are about 30,000 Hutterites comprising 300 colonies, living in the northwestern states and western Canadian provinces.

Amish Origins

The Amish (also called Plain People), were a much later subdivision (in 1693) of the Anabaptist movement. The Swiss division of the Mennonite branch of the movement in Europe was greatly aided through the efforts of one Jacob Ammann (also spelled Amman or Ammon), who later incited a split basically over the issue of shunning (avoiding fellowship with) excommunicated adherents. Little is known of Ammann's life except that he was born in Switzerland in the latter part of the 16th century, and later migrated to Alsace where he became a prominent Mennonite minister and church leader (Hostetler and Huntington, 1971). The Anabaptist practices about which he showed special concern included: the celebration of Holy Communion, which Ammann believed should be practiced twice annually instead of only once; the practice of foot-washing, which was not being observed consistently by some churches; and shunning *(Meidung)* which some congregations refused to acknowledge in the strict sense that Ammann proposed. Ammann believed that members should have absolutely nothing to do with excommunicated members. Excommunicated individuals should eat, sleep and live completely alone (Dyck, 1967). Two additional matters contributed to the resulting schism, namely, whether people accused of telling a falsehood should be excommunicated and whether true-hearted people (who were not necessarily declared believers) would be saved (Hostetler, 1977). When Ammann stated his position on these matters it was suggested that a meeting of church elders be called to discuss the impending debate. Ammann, however, wrote a warning letter on March 7, 1694, to Swiss ministers indicating that anyone who did not agree with him would be excommunicated even though he did not really have the authority to make such a statement. Of sixty-nine ministers who took sides in the division, twenty-seven sided with Ammann, twenty of them in Alsace. This area eventually became the European headquarters for the Amish movement even though the formal split was not realized until 1711.

From the very beginning the Amish became distinguishable from their fellowman through their insistence on conservative styles of clothing, the wearing of beards for married men, and their preference to substitute a hook-and-eye mechanism for fastening clothing instead of buttons. Initially, life was very difficult for these peasant farmers, but they endured. As Zook (1993), a Delaware Amish historian, describes it:

> There was not much chance in Germany or Switzerland for poor people to have many of life's comforts. They lived in crude houses often built with stone and sometimes with a roof of thatched straw. . . . Scattered through hills and valleys of not very fertile land, they were trusted by their neighbors, as no drunkards, gamblers or liars were among them. Observers saw love and respect between married people and their children (Zook, 1993, 81–82).

In church life the Swiss Amish, following Amman's dictates, strictly observed the practice of excommunication and shunning and settled for a form of local church government. Except for a very constricting interpretation of humility they held to other Anabaptist beliefs. This did not mean that they had much to do with other Anabaptist groups, for during their first century in Europe they kept pretty well to themselves. In fact, they literally developed a Mennonite subculture of their own (Fretz, 1989).

The Amish in Europe were subject to very severe persecution because their new faith forbad them to swear allegiance to the state. They were also unpopular because they refused to engage in military activities or any other violent act. Eventually some of them were burned at stake, and in one town a huge bonfire was built in the town square to accommodate all the local heretics. At Tun, Switzerland, in what is now Tun Castle, as many as 500 Amish were imprisoned at one time, awaiting their execution. When burning the "heretics" at stake attracted additional believers who also wanted to show themselves willing to die for their faith, the prisoners were executed by drowning. Their heads were stuck into a barrel of water and they were held down by two men until they drowned. These executions were held at night to minimize publicity about the event. Sometimes public burnings inspired other believers who were also willing to die for their faith. State officials feared that such attractions could let the movement get out of hand. Nearly one thousand Amish died for their faith in this way before the "offense" was abolished in 1571 (Zielinski, 1975). To celebrate the bravery of their ancestors, for many years Anabaptists read from only one other book besides the Bible, *Mirror of the Martyrs*, which contained stories of brave Anabaptists who went willingly to their deaths rather than denounce their Savior (Oyer and Kreider, 1989).

American Emigration

After the Reformation religious persecution was the cause of many migrations from Europe to North America, and the Amish were no exception. By the year 1700 the Amish were able to negotiate plans to leave Europe for the United States. The peak American immigration periods for Amish settlement were 1727–1770 and 1815–1860. The first known Amish settlement in North America was established in 1736 in Berks County, Pennsylvania, and the second in Lancaster County, Pennsylvania. Once established, like most frontier churches, the Amish met at irregular times for worship because their religious leaders travelled extensively to the various settlements. Eventually bishops were ordained in every district as each community gained a measure of economic stability. Although there were Mennonites living near some of the Amish settlements the two groups had very little interaction during the first half century of life in America community (Nolt, 1992).

It took the Amish well over two hundred years to come to the point where they could live virtually undisturbed by governmental authorities even though there are still occasional matters that arouse public attention today. Having settled the matter of their opposition to war, as in the case of the Quakers through the establishment of a form of alternative service, the last bastion to fall was that of the school. Keim (1975) reports 14 court cases between 1927 and 1972 between the Amish and the state over Amish failure to comply with compulsory school attendance laws. In this respect, since the USA Amish finally gained permission to operate independent schools in 1972, their communities feature one of the few truly synthesized forms of education in North America. That synthesis is identifiable in terms of what is taught in school closely complements the ongoings of the church and home life. A fuller treatment of the evolution of Amish schooling in America is offered in a later chapter. First it will be useful to consider a little of the history of the Amish in their first major settlement in Lancaster County, Pennsylvania.

Life in America

The state of Pennsylvania, in which Lancaster County is situated, was a part of the territory identified for the Dutch by Henry Hudson's 1609 excursion into Delaware Bay. The first permanent settlement, Gottenborg, was established on Tinicum Island in 1643 by a company of Swedes and Finns. With the remainder of the region, the little colony passed from the Swedes to the Dutch in 1655, then to the British in 1664. In 1680, Quaker William Penn petitioned for land in the New World for a Quaker colony. This was granted despite the fact that the Quakers were also a persecuted sect in England and no government or state official really wanted to accommodate them. Perhaps the authorities in these countries thought it might be preferable to get rid of the annoying pacifists. It was Philadelphia that became the seat of the minute Quaker kingdom which William Penn sought to establish, envisaging the future community as a "Holy City of Brotherly Love." By the time of the American Revolution, symbolized by the Declaration of Independence in 1776, three factions of people had been satisfactorily endorsed by Penn. First he made peace with the Indians by dealing with them honestly and scrupulously; second, he attracted a group of people now called the "Pennsylvania Dutch", including Amish, Mennonites, Dunkards, and Moravians from Germany; and third, there came a variety of other immigrants who were eager to live under the privileges and responsibilities outlined by Penn for the new colony, notably Scots and Irish.

Philadelphia today still shows the vestiges of Penn's dream for a city of peace as well as reflecting a very patriotic atmosphere. In the city one will find Independence Hall, home of the first American Congress; Liberty Bell which symbolizes the freedom for which Americans fought; Christ Church which was attended by many of the first American political leaders; and the largest Quaker meeting house in the United States, with a seating capacity of 1,200. A little west of the city is Valley Forge where the decisive battle between the half-trained American army and the invading British took place. Here one can walk in the footsteps of George Washington, Benjamin Franklin and William Penn and ponder what might have happened if the latter would have been able to fully develop his Holy City of Brotherly Love.

Lancaster County is less than a two-hour drive west of Philadelphia, and is surrounded on both sides by several significant historical sites. With Valley Forge on the east of it, indicating great beginnings for the country, Gettysburg is an hour to the west of Lancaster County by automobile and symbolizes the tragedy that can befall a great nation when "brother arises against brother," namely the Civil War. The site of the last great battle is now a park and contains more than a thousand statues erected by various American states and private organizations to commemorate the loss of 51,000 casualties in that bloody battle. Realistic portrayals of the final day of the slaughter conjure up the picture of General Robert E. Lee of the Confederacy marching across an open field with 15,000 of the best of the south against the booming cannons of the Union Army under General George Gordon Meade. In a matter of a very short time it was all over but the gathering of the dead and wounded amidst the feeling of horror brought about by the realization that a nation was a war with itself. Toward the culminating edge of the park is a monument, dedicated in memory of the war, and it was at this location that President Abraham Lincoln read his famous two-minute Gettysburg address, promising Americans that the nation would again achieve peace. Almost two years went by before that promise found fruition.

The City of Lancaster is the county seat, and advertises itself as the oldest inland city in America. It also features the first F. W. Woolworth five-cent store, and Fulton Theatre, which is America's longest running institution of that kind. The City of Lancaster calls itself "The Gateway to Amish Country." Lancaster can boast that the city was the capital of America for a single day, September 27, 1777, when Congress stopped there on its flight from Philadelphia after the Battle of Brandywine. It was also the state capital from 1799 to 1812.

Lancaster County Settlement

Lancaster County is considered the most productive agricultural area in the United States and is often called the "Garden Spot of America." Small, but lush farms dot the landscape, the average being only sixty to seventy acres in size. This is small by western North American standards, but production is unusually high because farmers can obtain as many as three crops of alfalfa in a year, or by a simple rotation of crops, increase the productivity of the soil. A fairly standard rotation would include corn or tobacco, wheat or barley, and potatoes or carrots, each grown for a single year.

Amish farmers are among the best in the county and their homes are usually identifiable by the use of the windmill or the famous waterwheel which furnishes a form of energy by its location on one of the many streams that occupy the county. The use of electricity or other modern forms of energy is frowned on by the Amish as is the use of the automobile for transportation. The Amish utilize mainly horse-drawn equipment for farming even though such machinery is sometimes exceedingly difficult to come by. As a result, Amish farmers sometimes outbid antique dealers for household and farm equipment at local auction sales. Similarly, Amish farms are rarely sold, and then mainly to other Amish, and when "English" farms are sold they are usually purchased by the Amish. The term "English" is used by the Amish to denote any groups other than themselves or Mennonites.

The Tourist Hard-Sell

It is the simple, traditional type of lifestyle of the Amish that draws the attention of nearly five million tourists who come to Lancaster County during the summer months of every year. Many are lured by the literature which advertises Amish life as "plain and simple". Local businessmen are prepared for the influx. To the Amish the tourist is sometimes annoying because the roads are filled with camera-laden people who will

Figure 2-1. Extended family living—Amish style.

stop at any convenient (or inconvenient) place on the road to "get a shot" of a horse-drawn buggy. Happy that they have finally reached "Dutch Country" tourists are often eager to buy anything that will remind them, that they has been in the land of the Plain People. One local enterprising business man covered a large number of wash-tubs with black paint and sold them over the summer months as "Amish washtubs". Reportedly, they went like hot-cakes. Bender (1995) describes the dilemma of Amish life constantly evaded by curious onlookers:

> This was their world, and we were voyeurs, looking at them with the same curiosity we might look at someone in a freak show. I hated it—and had to leave. "Are there any Amish communities where the people don't live in a fish-bowl?" I asked the surprised woman at the tourist bureau. She suggested a somewhat remote county several hours away in Ohio (19).

Many tourists do not realize when they enter Lancaster County's "Dutch Country" that there is little that is actually "Dutch" about it in the sense that the Netherlands are Dutch. Most of the original inhabitants of Lancaster County, including the Amish, were Swiss-Germans, not Dutch. It is quite possible that since the locals take liberties with the King's English in making translations from their dialect, they also equate the German word "Deutsche" with the English equivalent of "Dutch". Some Lancaster residents spell the word "Deitsch". In any event, the Amish comprise a unique community, and their favorable reputation is well established. Pennsylvania Dutch cooking is virtually second to none, and local folklore comprises a whole variety of interesting topics including superstitions, signs of the moon, marital tales, Zodiac beliefs, epitaphs and proverbs. Consider, for example, the following Pennsylvania Dutch home remedies and cures:

- To repair a hernia get a forged nail, drive it into a piece of wood and keep the wood in a dry place.
- To cure a person of alcoholism, scrape the dirt that collects under his fingernails and put it into his whiskey.
- To cure piles, carry horse-chestnuts in your pockets (Smith, 1976).
- To quit smoking, for 8 to 10 days drink only unsweetened fruit and vegetable juices. This will cleanse the system. This can be done each month, or whenever the temptation is strong. Couple this with earnest prayer and there is more strength to overcome. A complete fast helps also.
- To get rid of warts, rub each day with a piece of white chalk. Apply kerosene. Good for corns also. Cut milkweed to get the milky juice. Apply several times.
- To cure bedwetting, eat dandelion. This herb is good and may be added to other dishes such as soups and stews, etc. (Cart, 1988).

Pennsylvania Dutch proverbs and sayings include these gems:

- Old timers can recall when a fellow wondered where his next dollar was coming from, instead of where it had gone.
- The way to live with no money is to stay out of town, stay home, and make do with what is there (Byler, 1991).
- He who feeds well, churns well.
- A wife that does not know how to keep house throws out more with a teaspoon than a man can bring in with a shovel.
- He who digs a ditch for others falls in it himself.
- Kissing wears out—cooking don't (Smith, 1976).

Lancaster County merchants have made the most of their financial opportunity by the presence of the Amish in their midst, and there are motels, restaurants, museums, farming villages, places offering buggy rides, and a wide variety of pseudo-Amish artifact factories all over the county. No matter from which direction the county is entered, the visitor will encounter advertisements about "Amish Country". Many signs illustrate the extent to which Pennsylvania Dutch is literally translated into English in order to present the tourist with the flavor of a unique setting. Among the vacation spots to be frequented by the tourist are: The Mennonite Information Center, with its replica of the Hebrew Temple and the adjacent Mennonite Historical Society; the People's Place, featuring stores, an art gallery, a museum and a slide presentation on the Amish; and the National Wax Museum of Lancaster County Heritage, with lifelike reproductions of every Amish event from a barn-raising to a school classroom in action. The museum also accentuates local heroes, Davey Crockett and Daniel Boone, and the only Lancaster County-born president, James Buchanan. Other attractions include Old Strasburg and Traintown, The Amish Homestead, the Amish Farm and House featuring a "genuine Amish family", The Amish Village, and the Weavertown One-room Schoolhouse with moving wax replicas of Amish pupils. The Hans Herr House, erected in 1719, is in excellent condition and complete with the original large fireplace and oven and is well-deserving of a visit. The palate may be appeased at such establishments as the Plain and Fancy Farm and Restaurant, the Good and Plenty Restaurant, The Bird-in-Hand Motel or the Amish Barn. It is virtually impossible to travel in Lancaster County and not be reminded that this is indeed Amish country. Tourists with Mennonite background, of course, always take time to visit the world headquarters of the Mennonite Central Committee (a relief organization) in nearby Akron.

A County of Churches

The landscape of Lancaster County is rural yet urban-like because of the many small towns that exist only a few miles from each other. Churches are everywhere, as a result of the religious fervor which brought many of the original inhabitants to the county and which was later rekindled in the period of the "Great Religious Awakening" which swept that part of the United States in the latter part of the eighteenth century.

Lancaster County is the original American home of such groups as Quakers, Mennonites and Amish, Brethren, Moravians, Evangelicals and United Brethren. Church splits (and the occasional union) have been a fairly steady fare among most of these groups from the time of their founding to the present. As a result the visitor will be hard-pressed to differentiate among the various kinds of Brethren Churches or to know the difference between the Evangelical Congregational Church and the former Evangelical Association which merged with the United Brethren in 1946, and in 1968 joined the United Methodist Church. Similarly, while average citizens, lacking some knowledge of Anabaptist beginnings, will be uncertain as to the major differences between Amish and conservative Mennonites, to say nothing of more liberal Mennonite groups (often differentiated as "plain and fancy" by the Amish), it will be even more difficult for them to appreciate the reasons why some of the splinter groups have developed. Two Lancaster County researchers once compiled a listing of Mennonite and Amish groups in Lancaster numbering twenty-five in all, with memberships ranging from 12,000 for the Lancaster Mennonite Conference of Mennonites to ten members for the United Mennonite Church. Some of the church names in this list indicate geographical or personal derivations for their identity, for example, Old Order Mennonites (Pikers/Stauffers), Summit View Amish, Gap View Amish, Melita Fellowship and Unaffiliated Mennonite Church (Good and Good, 1979). Small wonder that local Mennonite and Amish Lancaster residents want to know which particular group one is talking about when one inquires about a particular characteristic.

Some of the reasons why some Mennonite or Amish church splits have occurred reveal particularistic thinking on behalf of the participants. The Funkites, for example, represented one of the first breaks with the Mennonite Church, separating over the issue of pacifism and the financing of the Civil War. Christian Funk, a local minister in Pennsylvania, believed that taxation had as its sole purpose the financing of war, and he wanted no part of it. Because of the obvious clashes his group inevitably had with governmental authorities, its growth was threatened from the very beginning. In 1811, which marked the death of their leader, the Funkites began to dwindle in number, after an existence of just over thirty years.

The Herrites are the "new Mennonites" who originated in the latter part of the 18th century, after the War of the Revolution. The original leader, Francis Herr, was expelled from the Mennonite Church for being too critical. After that he attracted a small group of adherents and addressed them in house meetings from a seated position because he had not been ordained, and thus did not deserve to preach from a standing position. After his death, his son, John, continued leadership giving voice to his concern for the abolition of worldly practices among believers such as attending county fairs, observing horse races, or engaging in drinking, jesting, voting or foolish talk. The group was initially known as Herrites or New Mennonites although they have formally adopted the name "Reformed Mennonites", and have less than 100 members in Lancaster County. Other congregations may be found in Ontario (Canada), Indiana, Illinois, Ohio, Michigan and New York. At its peak the denomination probably numbered between 2,000 and 2,500 members (Smith, 1979). Adherents like to claim that Milton Stavely Hershey, founder of the Hershey Chocolate Corporation, was raised in a Reformed Mennonite Church although he later married a non-Mennonite and left the church.

The Stauffer or "Piker" Mennonites are a group of buggy-type Mennonites whose name derives from the fact that they originally met in a building located on the Ephrata Pike and their first minister was Jacob Stauffer. The word "pike", by the way, refers to roads that were built of stones or rock rather than merely consisting of mud or sand. By 1832 there were 3,000 miles of "turnpike" in Pennsylvania.

The issue which caused the Stauffer group break from the Mennonite Church was the claim that the larger Mennonite Church was increasingly allowing worldliness to creep in, with Stauffer arguing that the church had lost her unique role in the community by ceasing to practice severe discipline on lax members. By 1936, nearly ninety years after the founding of the church, the Pikers could claim about 330 members. Today they comprise about three times that number with one congregation in Lancaster County having a membership of nearly 200. Stauffer people are forbidden to own cars and must wear simple clothing. Unlike many Amish groups, who cling to the hook-and-eye mechanism, the Stauffer people are allowed to use buttons on clothing. Staffer men do not wear beards and their women have their hair pinned up under a prayer cap.

Weaver Mennonites are exclusive to Lancaster County and their single congregation originated in 1916, breaking with the Stauffer Mennonites over the interpretation of the principle of nonconformity. At that time they numbered about a hundred with today's membership being less than 100. Their way of life is virtually identical to that of the Stauffer Mennonites in social practice and clothing styles.

For the student of Anabaptist church history details of break-ups and factionizing abound about groups of people who from the beginning wanted very much to fulfill with precision the injunctions of the Scriptures and thus believed it necessary to form unique groups. Such actions are exemplified by the Oberholtzer division of the Mennonite Church, which began in 1860 and which later joined the General Conference Mennonite Church, the split having been caused by the actions of young John H. Oberholtzer who thought that the Mennonite practice of wearing plain clothing was an outdated practice. He also held a more liberal view toward the courts and interaction with non-Mennonites. Ten years later another schism developed, this time with the General Conference Church, when William W. Gehman led a faction away to form the Evangelical Mennonite Church. The Brenneman group, which split from the Mennonite Church later than Gehman did, joined with Gehman and a group formed by Solomon Eby, all in the space of the 1870s, and the three factions formed the United Evangelical Mennonite Church. Still later, this union added a splinter group from the River Brethren (Brethren in Christ Church) and originated the Mennonite Brethren in Christ. Complicated, isn't it?

Still other church names, all in Lancaster County, and all within the Mennonite umbrella, are: the Wislerites and the Martinites, known for their tendency to maintain traditional ways above all else; the Wengerites, who oppose education for their children and cling to agriculture as the only means of livelihood; and the "Black-Bumper" or Horning Mennonites who originally allowed automobile ownership as long as the chrome parts were painted black in order to avoid pride of ownership. Today the tendency is simply to purchase cars with subdued colors and avoid having to use black paint.

One of the most interesting church splits in Lancaster County among Mennonites occurred in 1942 when the "Thirty-Fivers" or Reidenbach Mennonites formed in order to maintain a separation from the world. Originally there were (you guessed it) thirty-five of them, and they determined to be exact in instructing their youth where to draw the line in maintaining a pure Christian identity. The Reidenbach name is derived from the fact that their meeting house is near a store by that name. Unique features about the Thirty-Fivers include their refusal to use the windmill, let alone electricity, because they argue that "God gave us the water, but it would not be right to expect Him to pump it for us." They are also opposed to the use of rubber tires on buggies, the taking of photographs (as are the Amish), or the use of washing machines powered by gasoline, something which most Amish have since accepted. Ultra-conservative in life-style, the Thirty-Fivers use coal-oil lamps for lighting (they previously used only candles), refuse to use school buses for their children, and avoid the use of all modern machinery, for example, they allow manure to be spread by hand only. A full explanation of the various Amish and Mennonite subgroups in Lancaster County alone could fill a volume, so the foregoing are mentioned merely as representative of their communities.

Amish Lifestyle

Lancaster County Amish

To the untrained non-Mennonite eye, there is no difference between conservative Swiss Mennonites (often called Old Order Mennonites), and Amish unless one observes that the Amish drive grey buggies in Lancaster County and the conservative (Old Order) Mennonites drive black ones. Later one may notice that in parts of Pennsylvania there are also yellow and white buggies in use for specific identity reasons. Insofar as clothing and life-style are concerned, however, it will take more than a glance to determine the real differences among these various communities.

In Lancaster County the Amish are known as comprising three main categories:

(i)   the Old Order Amish, who cling to the traditional way of life featuring the use of the home as a church, the buggy, and the avoidance of electricity;

(ii)   the Beachy Amish (also called Church Amish, Amish Mennonite or Weavertown Mennonites), who allow electricity, telephones, tractors and automobiles although their cars are subdued in color; and,

(iii) The "New Amish", who represent a variety of departures from the Old Order (and often from each other) in that they may keep plain garb but allow cars, electricity, meeting houses or the relaxation of other particularistic regulations (Denlinger, 1981).

It is the Old Order Amish and conservative groups of Mennonites that attract tourist curiosity because of their obvious traits, namely the use of the horse-drawn buggy for transportation and their conservative dress. Only the serious visitor will discover that there is more to an Amish person than "meets the eye" in connection with family life, courtship and marriage, church practices and the well-publicized barn-raising. These practices will be described in more detail later on.

The Beachy Amish present an enigma to many people because of their curious practice of mixing the old and the new. Like most Mennonites, they sing in four-part harmony, something which Old Order Amish are forbidden to do because of the distraction it would cause from concentrating on "singing unto the Lord". In some Amish schools children do sing in two-part harmony as we ourselves witnessed. Beachy Amish originated in 1927, from among the Old Order Amish, under the leadership of Bishop Moses M. Beachy who saw little wrong with the practice of Sunday School, church buildings, and the use of the automobile and electricity. By the 1930s the movement had spread to other states. Conservative beliefs in the fellowship include reservations about detailed records and the compiling of statistics. Frequently comments are heard about the census of King David in the Old Testament and the resulting displeasure of God with the king. The late Bishop Jonas Herschberger of Montezuma, Georgia, did not keep a record of the number of couples he married, individuals he baptized or ministers whom he ordained. His underlying purpose was to be faithful to his calling (Yoder, 1987). Eventually this movement grew to about ninety congregations who, though not formalized into a conference, do function as a separate denomination (Hostetler, 1977). In 1955 the group formed the Amish Mennonite Aid, a Beachy mission, relief and service organization. In 1970 they established Calvary Bible School at Calico Rock, Arkansas and began a monthly church periodical named the *Calvary Messenger* (Nolt, 1992). The Beachy Amish also operate their own information center in Lancaster County as a means of acquainting visitors with their way of life and the Christian faith.

The New Amish groups began to emerge in the middle of the late 1960s in both Pennsylvania and Ohio for basically two reasons. One was the appeal of modern technology for farming and transportation, and the second was a spiritual concern about "cleansing of wrong ways". Adherents to the New Amish community began to speak of the "assurance of salvation", implying that it was time to speak out about their Christian experiences. Old Order Amish bishops warned them that to do so was an act of pride but they would not refrain. The Old Order Amish teaches that it is impossible to have assurance of salvation; at best the Christian can only hope for this event or state as a gift from God (Hostetler, 1993).

Members of the New Amish community also spoke out on other fronts, for example the growing and use of tobacco. They argued that it was contradictory of some Old Order communities to grow the weed and then forbid its use to their members. Some of the new Amish groups do not permit the use of automobiles or meeting houses; others again utilize pretty well every modern convenience, such as power-driven generators for cooling bulk milk, telephones and modern plumbing. At best it is wise to approach each separate group with the intent of learning their own particular explanation for their conduct rather than analyzing or even criticizing it from a lack of knowledge.

Old Order Amish Customs

The Lancaster Amish population, like that of any other area, is divided into church districts numbering from about one hundred baptized souls, who meet in their homes for worship, on a rotating basis, on alternate Sundays. This procedure arose during the persecution period in Europe as a means of confusing their tormentors as to the location of the worship services.

The Ordnung

Central to the lifestyle of the Amish is the authority of church leaders called the *Ordnung*. All members of the church must gain approval from the local church leaders for acts of behavior, which are not already the norm in their particular group, or face excommunication and shunning. That which is permissible is well known by church adherents even though such rules are never written down. It is up to individual members to be aware of all regulations and taboos. Members of the *Ordnung* meet twice a year, before Communion Sunday, to discuss and/or amend the existing regulations, or to consider individual cases of possible indiscretion. Rules do not necessarily correspond in every detail from one church district to another, but this lack of consistency concerning minor issues does not seem to bother the adherents. Their object is to live a simple lifestyle (preferably agrarian) under the blessing of the church. Thus when an Amish family relocates to another Amish settlement or community it would be essential that they immediately appraise themselves of any local doctrinal idiosyncrasies. An articulation of the basic requirements for obtaining "the good life" and thereby gaining community approval, is neither an Amish orientation nor concern, and that alone seems to bother outsiders to an unwarranted extent. "Why don't the Amish ever question the rules?" they ask. "Can't they see the inherent contradictions in their system?" One intended objective of local guidebooks to answer obvious questions for tourists such as, "Why do Amish separate themselves from the modern world? Why do a gentle people shun disobedient members? Why is ownership of cars objectionable, but not their use? Why are tractors permitted around barns but not in fields? Why are horses instead of tractors used to pull modern farm, machinery? Why do Amish use the services of professionals— lawyers, doctors and dentists—and oppose higher education? (Kraybill, 1990a). Good and Good (1979) have come to the rescue by entitling their guidebook, *20 Most Asked Questions About Amish and Mennonites.* Scott (1981) has devoted an entire volume to explaining why the buggy is the only acceptable means of transportation among the Amish, and another volume (1986) to explaining why Amish dress the way they do. On the issue of the automobile, for example, the Amish show an interesting stance; while it would be wrong to own one, they do ride buses or ride in someone else's car if the distance is too great to be travelled by buggy. They often hire a car and driver (usually a Mennonite) to travel to other Amish settlements in the USA. They see a great difference between using something and owning it.

Amish World-view

More than anything, tourist-type questions represent a only a vague understanding of the Amish Weltanschauung or World-view. The Amish objective is to live as traditional a life as possible, using the advances of technology or modern value systems only when the traditional way *must* be amended. For example, when an Amish individual is no longer able to purchase "antique" farm implements for his horse-drawn operation he may use a horse-drawn wagon to pull an engine around the field, letting the engine operate the newer machine he has had to purchase in order to stay in business. This way is not breaking any of the rule of the *Ordnung,* and chances are that he has checked out beforehand with the *Ordnung* the "legitimacy" of his new arrangement.

Amish life holds many surprises for the outsider who easily comes to the conclusion that the Amish are a backward or "out of it" people. Quite to the contrary there are a number of modern literary pursuits among the Amish. For example, some Amish are artists, and their wares are available to tourists. Various crafts such as appliqued and embroidered quilts, which show a high degree of artistic finesse, are also available— complete with the artist's signature. In the home of an Amish bookbinder in Lancaster County there is the beginning of a local Amish Historical Society with an elaborate collection of old books and records. At the Amish print shop in Gordonville one can obtain copies of the Minutes of the National Old Order Amish Steering Committee dating from October 1966. This committee meets several times annually in different locations across the United States and deals with matters of concern to Amish people generally such as the military draft or schooling. The grammar and sentence structure of these reports might easily startle a good English teacher but the intended meaning is clear. Consider the following statement on conscription:

> The present draft was briefly explained by the Chairman and it was said the draft is not dead but only sleeping. They can not at this time compulsory call [sic] up any boys but they are only getting 48% of the boys desired by voluntary means (*Minutes of Old Order Amish Steering Committee from October 24, 1973 to October 22, 1980,* 2).

The Amish in America and in Waterloo County, Ontario, where migrations occurred in the early nineteenth century, generally keep in touch with each other through a national publication, *The Budget*, which contains news items submitted by local correspondents, letters from individuals, or information of concern to the people generally. In operation for more than a century, *The Budget* is published in Sugar Creek, Ohio, and an annual subscription may be purchased for a nominal fee. It is privately-owned by non-Amish, but its arrival in an Amish mailbox is eagerly anticipated. A collection of letters to *The Budget* has been printed under the title, *I Saw it in the Budget* (Yoder, 1990). The letters contain many personal messages and portray thoughts of worry, sorrow or homesickness or descriptions of treatment by residents in various Amish communities Note the following letters commenting on the role of *The Budget*:

The Budget is a unique paper. There is perhaps no other paper quite like it. Many of us are dependent upon it for news of our people throughout the greater part of the United States. — *Milverton, ON*

I hear some folks have some queer ideas about *The Budget*. They would not subscribe to it, but still they are anxious to read it. For my part, if I would not like it I would not spend much time reading it. I never look it over but what I find some interesting letters or items about relatives of friends, and what is not interesting to me is to somebody else. I would rather read *The Budget* than worldly papers. — *Amish, IA*

I wrote my first letter to *The Budget* in May, 1900. . . . Was a regular correspondent with the exception of a few years when I failed in writing as I had lost my health, lost courage and was so discouraged I could not do much. But must say, the Bible and *The Budget* are my pastime in lonely hours. I can read *The Budget* every week. Always news and nearly every letter in *The Budget* I can read of some I know and had lost track of them. You find your old friends through *The Budget* — *Middlefield, OH*

The Budget is an Amish institution. It satisfies the need to know what is generally happening in other Amish districts and, more importantly, is an approved channel of inter-district communication. Some letters or reports are exceeding brief, yet poignant. For example:

Last night we attended the singing (Mill Creek at Christ Millers). It is estimated that there were about 325 young folks there. — *Bird-in-Hand, PA*

Sam K. Stolzfuz had an ice-cream supper for employees and some friends on Thursday evening; also a fine lot of fire works. — *Gordonville, PA*

I learned through *The Budget* that my old friend, Christian Ginerich, has gone to the spirit land. — *Flanigan, IL*

Those girls who were out scouting some time ago put me in mind of some starving cows, which hunger forces to break their lines to see some green pastures. — *Nappannee, IN*

It has been reported that David B. Schrock, formerly of this place, has captured a dear [loved one] in Lancaster Co. [sic]. — *Arthur, IL*

Generally speaking, the Amish are not an evangelistic community in the sense that they seek to attract others to their cause. They do allow people to join their ranks, but this stance is perhaps more indicative of cultural conversion than a religious experience. There are at least two family names, Stoltzfus (formerly an English name, "Proudfoot"), and Huyard (a French derivation) drafted into the Amish family tree, one by the adoption of a twelve-year old boy and the other through adult conversion. Apparently an Englishman named Proudfoot came to live with the Amish and later married an Amish woman. His name was promptly translated into the German and Lancaster County has many residents by that name as a result (Friesen, 1983)

Communication among the Amish, nationally, is important enough that they have published a shop and service directory of Old Order businesses which lists Amish businesses across the United States. The directory contains the names and addresses of blacksmiths, furniture factories and stores, buggy shops, cabinet makers and a wide variety of other enterprises.

Amish Beliefs

Instead of being a people who merely cling to the traditional way of living for its own sake, the Amish hold to very definite beliefs regarding social organization and religion. Fundamentally Anabaptist, the following represent principles unique to the Old Order Amish.

First, Amish life is founded on the attitude of absolute submission to the *Ordnung*. When a person is under investigation for a possible misdeed, there is no thoroughness that matches the fervor of the investigating elders. John A. Hostetler, now retired from Temple University, was raised in an Amish family, and describes the submission aspect of the community in his book, *Amish Society*, under the subtitle, "Rigidity and The Illusion of Gentleness" (Hostetler, 1993). While the Amish are friendly to outsiders and give the impression of being a "gentle people", their treatment of their own kind when misconduct is in question is often the harshest kind possible. Amish life, then, is grounded in implicit obedience.

Second, the Amish perceive the traditional way of doing things as the best. When modernity foists itself on them they resist as long as possible but they will go along with change insofar as they have to, no more. Ironically, the Anabaptist sources from which they sprang, rejected all tradition in the church and emphasized a direct obedience to the Scriptures. Some Amish, it seems, reverse the importance of tradition with obedience to the Scriptures. Herschberger (1992) tells the story about a family who moved from Iowa to Indiana and started studying the Bible on their own. They attended a Beachy Amish Church and were soon visited by the husband's father from Iowa who wanted to know why they were leaving the Old Order Church.

The son replied, "Well, we have been reading and studying our Bible and decided to change". "Well, don't read your Bible so much and listen to your bishop more," said the father. The son went into the other room, picked up his Bible, returned to the room they were in and laid it on the table saying, "If you don't want me to read the Bible, you take the book with you." The father walked to the table, paused, looking down at the Book of Life but he couldn't take the good book with him (31–32).

Amish regulations govern all aspects of living, including how to make a living. While most Amish farm, there are many communities where this vocation is limited. In those instances individuals may work for wages, but only in approved outlets. Amish farms are usually about 80 acres in size and rarely do they need more land than that. Amish farmers use a careful rotation of crops to feed back into the soil the exact nutrients required for the next crop and keep the land fruitful. A corn crop is followed by oats, and in the fall when oats are harvested, the stubble is plowed and wheat is sowed along with legume seeds. When the wheat is harvested, the stubble is mowed and the next spring and summer, several cuttings of hay are made and the hayfield is pastured in the fall. During the winter the sod is manured, and in late winter or early spring the sod is plowed and in May planted again to corn (Kline, 1990). This careful manipulation of the soil shows a reverence for the land and guarantees its perpetual production.

Figure 2-2. Amish farm.

Figure 2-3. Buggy style—open cart.

Third, nonconformity with the world is stressed as an all-inclusive principle encompassing dress, manner of transportation and economic aspects. It is this principle that confuses visitors to Lancaster County because they sense elements of nonconformity which appear to contradict the commands of the *Ordnung*. A case in point is the telephone which the Old Order Amish are forbidden to have in their homes. There are farms, however, that do have a telephone with the approval for its use because it is necessary to their operation; however, it must be appropriately camouflaged. Hence, the phone is relegated to an "outhouse-like" construction at the side of the road, away from the house. Apparently this arrangement discourages continual use of the device and encourages the "for business only" habit. This kind of arrangement may not be approved in every congregation, however, because approval and restrictions regarding any form of behavior are often unique to a specific church district. Amish businessmen who rely on use of the telephone have obtained permission for its use and a recent study (Kraybill and Nolt, 1995) report that 91 percent of Amish businessmen employ the telephone on a regular basis.

A *fourth* principle of Amish life is basic, albeit very conservative Christianity. If one takes the time to weed out the various traditions and cultural trappings of the Plain People, one will discover a serious intent to follow the teachings of Jesus Christ. In this pursuit they, like other mainline Christian churches, are probably imperfect, but this does not mean that their discipleship is any less valid in quality. They may not impress anyone with their indifference to evangelicalism, but neither will anyone be able to accuse them of fostering superstar Christianity or of seeking to build massive religious empires. On the other hand, their brotherly love is freely extended to persons in need, and is classically observable in the famous barn-raising event. When an Amish barn burns down, and this appears to happen at least once or twice a year somewhere in the neighborhood, the Amish descend on the farm in question in full force. The men work to erect a new structure under the supervision of a head carpenter, selected from their own midst or someone acknowledged in that trade, and the women prepare food. The event is one of the most enjoyable social occasions for the Amish as there is much visiting and eating and the playing of practical jokes. Frequently the barn is completed in a single day.

Excommunication and Shunning

Many of the divisions that emerged among Anabaptist groups are explanatory on the grounds that the movement is grounded in a principle conducive to splintering, namely the principle that the believer is his own priest. Many of the early Anabaptist leaders took liberties with this doctrine and perceived themselves to be priests in the traditional sense of being responsible for the people who followed them. A wide variety of issues caused church divisions, but none was as pronounced as the issue of shunning excommunicated persons (Warner and Denligner, 1969).

The Biblical basis which the Amish utilize for the practice of the ban (shunning) is: "But now I am writing to you that you must not associate with anyone who calls himself a brother but is sexually immoral or greedy, an idolater or a slanderer, a drunkard or a swindler. With such a man do not even eat" (I Corinthians 5:11, NIV). Most Mennonites, to this day, have interpreted this text in a spiritual sense indicating that with people of the nature described above, one would not have enough in common to build a close friendship. Jacob Ammann, however, chose a very literal explanation even to the extent of requiring that a person was forbidden to have sexual relations with his or her spouse if the latter had been excommunicated. Thus, when a man was excommunicated his wife would usually opt for the same status in order to live freely with her husband. This severe form of the belief is not adhered to today although relatives who have been excommunicated are required to eat at a separate table if they continue to live at home. Weddings, for example, can be very complex activities if they are attended by excommunicated relatives. Usually two tables are set for a meal and the "guilty" persons accommodate their orthodox relatives by sitting where they are bidden. In business matters the process may become even more difficult because devout Amish are not allowed to receive any object directly from the hand of an excommunicated person. Many former Amish people simply accommodate their friends by placing the object in question on a table or other convenient location so that the "devout" person may pick it up without becoming contaminated. The practice gets a little difficult at times, particularly when the situation is a restaurant or grocery store. Excommunicated women who work as waitresses in local restaurants occasionally avoid serving their orthodox acquaintances simply to make things easier for them. Beachy Amish, by the way, do not practice shunning.

Violations which cause excommunication are usually noted by church leaders and guilty parties are asked to confess their sin before the congregation. One man was excommunicated when he refused to show repentance for the fact that he had permitted 37 bus loads of tourists to visit his farm over the summer. Had this happened on a smaller scale involving perhaps only one carload of visitors, the offence might have been unnoticed or gone unheeded. Having hundreds of non-Amish on one's home territory, however, must have looked to the religious authorities like the owner was attempting to draw attention to himself or to his possessions. It was that intimation which caused that particular behavior to become offensive.

Parenthetically, it is interesting that while the Amish are indirectly responsible for drawing millions of tourists to Lancaster County each year, they do not assume any responsibility for that phenomenon. Their concept is to live life in as isolationist a fashion as possible and if that causes curiosity, it is no concern of theirs. In the meantime they continue to contend with the inconvenience of curious and often intrusive tourists—who also like to purchase Amish goods.

In an interview with a previous Amish member, the process of excommunication in his former church was explained in terms of three stages. The first is initiated in the case of a minor violation such as having too fancy a buggy or engaging in an infraction of the dress code. The second stage, involving a more serious offence, requires three confessions of the fault, once every two weeks, for six weeks. If these are not forthcoming, or if they are judged to be lacking in sincerity, the third stage, namely excommunication, is undertaken. If the accused person appears fully repentant he or she is taken back into the fellowship of the church. The rite of re-entry is performed at the front of the church with the persons seeking reinstatement on their knees before the bishop.

Excommunicating a person is a very formal process among the Amish, and according to one source, this is the way the process was enacted with regard to his own ousting. The offence that this person and his wife were guilty of was to attend evangelistic meetings of a well-known Mennonite preacher in Lancaster County. The couple became aware that they were under fire when they were especially invited to church one day by one of the ministers. Since they were regular attenders, this special invitation was obviously a kind of warning of things to come. Once in church, they were invited to sit on the front bench where usually only the minsters sat, and soon the interrogation began. Instead of wanting to argue with the authorities, since that would be interpreted as belligerence, the man simply answered by defending his actions, and left the meeting. Later he was sent a registered letter which he refused to accept. Had he acknowledged it, the formality of excommunication would have been enacted. Still later, he was visited by two ministers of the church who tried to read the contents of the registered letter to him. He refused to listen and went to the kitchen of his home and locked the door. This way he could not hear the words of the letter being read. Since his wife had not been the subject of the excommunication process, the two ministers later returned to the house to read the woman a letter of excommunication, but when she heard the opening sentence she fled to the bathroom. The couple later began attending a Mennonite church and prided themselves on the fact that they had never been formally excommunicated by the Amish. They were, however, shunned by the members of the congregation involved.

An Ohio physician relates an experience he had with a conservative Amish family that shows the intensity with which excommunication and shunning are feared. This doctor frequently makes house calls to Amish homes, and one day when he received an urgent call from an Amish father about a sick child. Because the doctor's office was exceptionally busy, the doctor asked the family to bring the child to his office. The father refused and the doctor suggested that the man obtain the services of a car and driver and bring their child in that way. The father grew very upset and said if the physician did not come out immediately the child would die. The doctor then sent his nurse to the home who returned with the sick child and his mother. A week later, the doctor met a neighbor to the man who had called and asked why the man would not bring his sick child to the clinic. "Oh," the neighbor replied, "he's been going to the horse races again, traveling by car, and the bishop told him that if he was seen travelling in car again for any reason, he would be subject to very severe church discipline" (Lehman, 1994, 12–13).

Shunning is undoubtedly an effective tool for keeping a society intact even though it is not necessarily practiced with a great deal of consistency by the Amish. Some of the more moderate congregations ceased its practice with regard to persons who kept themselves in good standing in local Mennonite churches. Others attempted to retain shunning with the same fervor that the founder, Jacob Ammann, did when he excommunicated dozens of ministers who did not agree with him on the issue of shunning. On the positive side of the phenomenon is the Christian act of charity which the Amish bestow on a fully repentant soul—namely total forgiveness. As one former Amish individual put it, "You may have to go through a great deal of turmoil in achieving reinstatement, but when it happens, you know you have been forgiven!"

Forgiveness does not always come easily, however, as Schreiber, (1990) reports in a story that occurred in 1947 concerning the Andrew J. Yoder family of Ohio whose teenage daughter was stricken with poliomyelitis. Yoder had applied to the local bishops for permission to buy a car in which to take his daughter to the hospital for regular treatments. The bishops refused, but Yoder bought an automobile and subsequently withdrew his membership from the Old Order church. He then took up with a local conservative Mennonite group. Despite this action, he and his family were promptly excommunicated and shunned. Yoder's business, which somewhat relied on Amish customers, promptly suffered and Yoder sued church bishops, John J. Nisley and John W. Helmuth, for unfair treatment, not usually an Amish or Mennonite custom. He won his case while, ironically, the bishops in question travelled to the court house in rented automobiles. When the bishops refused to pay the required $5,000 fine, some property of Bishop John Helmuth was confiscated by the court (enough to pay half of the fine), sold, and paid to Yoder. When the Bishop Nisley was faced with paying his half of the fine, an anonymous non-Amish businessman stepped in and paid it for him. Not much later both bishops died and so did Yoder's young daughter. No one seemed to have gained from the incident and Yoder continued to be shunned by the Amish.

The Amish people say that it is always a delight to receive persons back into the order who have left the Church and tried out life in the other world. Many individuals who have experienced both excommunication and reinstatement would concur with this statement. Many, however, do not return because they find life in a conservative Mennonite denomination similar to the lifestyle they abandoned. Youth who leave the Old Order and who have not previously become baptized members, of course, do not face the hardship of shunning and are thus better able to retain family ties.

Amish Leadership

It is not the intention here to convey the impression that excommunication and shunning are activities which the Amish yearn to enact; on the contrary, they are considered a final resort when all else fails in bringing a straying person back into the ranks. These behaviors represent acts of serious spiritual significance, and no one enjoys their enactment nor the implications of such action. Ministers who constitute the *Ordnung* dread both the call to the ministry and the tasks which they must perform. It is not an office to which many young men aspire.

The selection of ministers among the Amish is not complicated, but it is a weighty process. Only men may be considered candidates for the office and they are not required to have any formal educational preparation beyond completion of the eighth grade which is that attained by the average Amish person. When an older minister retires or dies, nominations for his successor are called for from among the male members of the local congregation. Any man receiving at least three nominations is included in the final part of the selection process. This happens in the following manner: the presiding bishop gives a closed copy of the Bible to every eligible nominee, one of which has a slip of paper in it. After prayers are said, the candidates are instructed to open their Bibles at a certain place, and the candidate who finds a slip of paper in the copy he has is declared the new minister. Until this act occurs, no one knows just who the new leader will be.

The selection of a new minister puts a great deal of fear into the hearts of men who are nominated for the task as well as that of their wives, for few men really want the job. Still, if the congregation sees fit to give enough credence to a young man's character so as to include him on the list of nominees, it is not his choice to refuse. When the final step in the selection process is complete, the entire congregation present offers prayers for the new minister and there is much weeping and sadness of expression. At the same time the young man is assured of the congregation's support, and as a new member of the *Ordnung*, has the added charge of becoming mature enough to help make decisions that will affect the future life of the community.

After his selection, the new minister will be given a year or so to begin to prepare short sermons to present to the church and to participate in other rituals. Eventually he will graduate to the point of taking charge of a worship service and delivering the longer of the two Sunday morning sermons which may last up to two hours.

Courtship

When a young Amish man goes courting, and this is allowed with young women from the age of sixteen, he dresses up his buggy beyond the point of *Ordnung* regulations, since these rules may not apply directly to unbaptized males, and looks for a prospective partner at the Sunday night hoedown. Of course a couple cannot be married before they are church members so the fancy buggy will have to be "unadorned" prior to the day that the marital vows can be taken. Extra items that may have to go are decorated harnesses, bright lights (run with a 12 volt battery carried on the buggy), or maybe even a radio. Apparently these paraphernalia attract some young Amish women more than plain buggies do. Incidentally, state law now requires flashing lights on all buggies because of the high accident rate caused by driving in faster automobile traffic. Having spotted a desirable date, the young man asks if he may accompany her home. If she consents, a courtship may evolve. One elderly Amish man related how he had selected his wife when she was only fifteen years old. Thus it was when he took her home in his buggy she insisted on being let out at the gate. Later, when she was of courting age he was allowed into the living room to converse with his new-found love. As the custom is, Amish parents make themselves scarce for the courtship by vacating the living room early on Sunday night. Usually they will not even know whom their daughter or son is marrying until the announcement is read in the church several weeks before the wedding. This strikes outsiders as totally unbelievable, but to have it any other way, apparently, would heap a large amount of unwanted teasing on the head of the persons involved.

A traditional practice among the Amish, although it is denied by many today, was bundling or bed-courtship, because it gave an opportunity for a young man and his fiance to converse in order to get to know one another better (Smith, 1974). Sometimes a young man might have to travel many miles to see his fiance and it would be impossible to make it home for the night. The arrangement was also quite necessary because most early American homes consisted of little more than one room and there was little opportunity for courting couples to have privacy (Aurand, 1938). Hence they were allowed to lie on a bed together, fully clothed, for the purposes of talking. Sometimes the custom called for a rolled up blanket or plank to be laid between them but this was the exception rather than the rule. Also, since the rest of the entire family was trying to sleep in the same room it was felt to be a compromise measure for needed privacy. The practice has apparently been abandoned.

After several months of courtship an Amish couple will obtain permission from the local minister for permission to marry. On receiving consent, an announcement will usually be made orally in church for two weeks; soon the family and the community will swell with excitement about the coming event because weddings are a very festive occasion.

The following description of an Amish wedding was written by Aaron S. Glick who was raised in an Amish home and later served as a guide for the Mennonite Information Center in Lancaster County. It is herewith generously paraphrased with his permission.

The Amish Wedding

When colorful autumn leaves begin to fall, crops have been harvested, and November is just around the corner—the young Amish couples are ready for their weddings.

According to Amish tradition in Lancaster County, weddings are held on Tuesdays or Thursdays, mostly during November. (Some have to be held in December since there are now too many weddings for the available Tuesdays and Thursdays of November). This leaves the Monday or the Wednesday before the wedding for preparation for the occasion.

To comply with Pennsylvania law, Amish couples go to the Lancaster County Court House to apply for marriage licenses. To comply with Amish tradition, their intention to marry is announced several weeks ahead of their wedding date by the deacon during a regular Sunday worship service. After that announcement, a young man will drive his horse and buggy from farm to farm to invite those whom the bride's parents would like to honor by having them attend the ceremony and feast held at the home of the bride.

The Amish bride usually makes her own wedding dress and buys identical materials for her attendants. Navy blue, mauve and other dark shades of cloth are typical colors for the wedding dress. The bride and her entourage also wear white caps and aprons although in some church districts the preferred color is black for caps. No one in the wedding party carries flowers (Scott, 1988). Some time is needed for the bride's family to prepare for the wedding feast (consisting of two meals) for as many as 300 to 400 guests. Most of the cooking is done the day before the wedding. It is customary for the relatives and friends to take an active part in helping with the preparation and serving of the meals. The parents of the bride do not work on the wedding day. Close relatives and friends take over.

Some guests will have to get up early on the wedding day. They may have as far as 20 miles to travel in their buggies, unless they have an opportunity to travel by car; and services usually begin at 8:30 a.m. For the worship service and ceremony, the guests sit on the plain wooden benches used for all Amish worship services. They will be in every available spot on the first floor. The service which lasts the entire morning—until 12:00 noon or 12:30, is opened by singing several German hymns in the traditional slow tunes (resembling a Gregorian Chant). There are always two sermons. The first is followed by a silent prayer in which the entire congregation kneels. The second sermon, or "main service", is conducted by the bishop who also performs the marriage. The ceremony is simple; the bride and groom promise to be faithful to each other "bis der Todt uns scheide" (till death do us part). There are no wedding bands nor flowers. When the ceremony ends, guests stand outside and wait until tables are set up and furnished in the same room where the marriage took place.

The feasting will require several settings at the long tables. At noon it will consist of roast chicken or turkey with filling, mashed potatoes, gravy, cooked vegetables, relishes, pickles, raw celery, potato chips, cakes, pies, and other desserts in abundance. The evening meal usually consists of fried chicken, candied sweet potatoes with splendid additions. The flavor and abundance of this food would be the envy of our regular society if it were known.

The newlyweds sit at one big table, known as the "corner table", with their attendants and other young couples who have recently been married as well as others who are still in the dating stage. The time following the noon and evening meal will be spent at the tables singing German hymns.

After the wedding day, the newlyweds will each live separately with both their respective parents during the week. During the winter they will then begin a series of weekend visits, with other married couples, to the homes of their close relatives and friends who were invited to their wedding. It is during these visits that they will receive gifts of kitchen utensils and other items that will be useful for the new home they will establish when spring comes. Most Amish couples prefer farming as a vocation, but in many cases the young man will need to work off the farm until enough money has been saved and a farm becomes available.

If a young Amish couple is fortunate enough to be able to work on his father's farm after marriage, an annex may be added to the present house in order to make room for the young couple. Some Amish farm homes have three or even more roomy additions, each added on as the need arose, featuring three or more different generations. One of these suites may be inhabited by the grandfather and grandmother of the family and is called the "Grossdadi (grandfather) house". Here they are allowed to live until their death or until they are unable to fend for themselves in which case their children will care for them. They may help with the chores occasionally, but will not be required to do so when their health fails. Few societies have as caring an atmosphere for elderly people as the Amish do.

Amish Home Life

The Amish are a people of seclusion. They prefer to have as little to do with the outside world as possible. Most household responsibilities are defined by age and sex although there is also a considerable degree of overlap in the work of a husband and wife. Only about 3 percent of married Amish women work outside the home (Kraybill, 1990b). The husband is seen as the spiritual head of the household and he is responsible for its spiritual welfare. He makes the final decisions as to matters related to church and interaction with the outside world. Sometimes the husband will assist his wife with garden and household chores and she, in turn, will help him with outside work. Many Amish women push lawn mowers, milk cows, gather eggs, and pull tobacco plants in the spring, stripping leaves from tobacco stalks in the winter. These chores are often a part of the woman's routine when her children are young. A women's main chores include looking after a household of children, cooking, sewing, mending, cleaning, washing, preserving food and supervising yard work. The kitchen is the center of an Amish woman's life. It is where everyone eats and where the days activities are discussed. The kitchen is plain by today's standards. Sometimes an oil-cloth may decorate the table, but most often it is bare. Regular dishes are of a plain heavy china, sometimes purchased at an auction. Painted tomato cans filled with houseplants may be placed on window sills, and a few embroidered pieces may be on view (Randle, 1992). It is a plain room with simple attachments, but it is home, and the heart-beat of Amish home life.

An Amish woman's work is sometimes made a little easier, for example with the introduction of the gasoline-powered washing machine. While rejecting electricity as a power source, many Amish have accepted battery-powered devices. All but the most conservative groups permit battery-run clocks, watches and flashlights. Electric shavers, calculators and buggy lights are similarly ignited, as are battery-operated electric fences. Some Amish dairy farms have complied with milk company requirements that they use battery-powered agitators in bulk tanks. Some Amish utilize solar generators to recharge these batteries (Scott and Pellman, 1990).

A widely-known Amish woman's art is quilting. This activity allows opportunities for socializing (the quilting bee) as well as a demonstration of skill and the quelling of aesthetic urges. Quilting has sometimes been viewed as a "salvage art" because it often allows the use of small scraps of material that are quite useless for other purposes. Quilting has survived among the Plain People because it is also a functional activity. Amish quilts may be purchased by tourists in almost every Amish community across the nation. Even though a quilt may be a "good one", and folded away in the bedroom chest except for use on Sundays and special holidays, the fact remains that it *will* sometime be used. As Pellman and Ranck (1981) suggest:

> A quilt legitimately displays a woman's ability as a seamstress, quilter, and color coordinator. She may show her quilts for the admiration of relatives and friends without intimidation. These reflect on her personality as does a well-kept home, lawn or garden (8).

In Amish country, Sunday is a day of rest. It may well be the institution that keeps the community together. On the day of worship the Amish try to do only unavoidable chores such as feeding livestock and milking cows. Even cooking is limited, although coffee and milk may be heated. Many Amish do not send milk to the creamery on Sundays, and if rain should threaten a crop, it will still not be harvested on the Sabbath (Schreiber, 1990). Sunday travel is restricted, and services are held every other Sunday. Those Sundays on which services are not held time is spent in visiting, fellowship and exchanging" local gossip". Men visit mostly about farms, crops and weather and the "weightier" subjects of government regulations, education, highway safety and even international affairs. Women seek a break from the monotony of daily routines to discuss family, gardens, children and what they "read in *The Budget*".

When it becomes the family turn to host church services a series of benches are brought in to accommodate the congregation. The seats are hard, services are long, and there may not even be enough places for everyone to sit down. The service itself is characterized by utter simplicity. There are no musical interludes, no collections are taken and there are no musical instruments. Sermons are relevant to local Amish life, and preachers often draw parallels between the activities of biblical characters and their own ancestors. When the service is over a formal communal meal is offered, with men and women sitting across the table from one another, but engaging in only minimal conversation.

Most Amish homes look as though they belong in the world of early America; they are almost entirely void of modern conveniences such as radios, television, electrical kitchen gadgetry, and the like. Since Amish men and women periodically mix their traditional roles, most Amish women do not spend a lot of time cooking creatively. Their cooking is often done "on the run" as they are frequently required to help in the fields or the barn with necessary chores. One young woman said that her family's day consisted of making 100 crocks of apple butter and corn husking. Even then, "there was still the whole house to clean" (Nolt, 1992, 193). Another female Amish youth noted that her day included washing clothes while her mother did the patching, her father cared for livestock and her brothers worked in the blacksmith shop.

An Amish breakfast usually consists of traditional "Amish reliables" such as eggs, fried potatoes, fried mush and scrapple. The noon meal might include meat and mashed potatoes, gravy, noodles and vegetables. Applesauce is sometimes served as a salad. The evening meal is similarly "heavy", and may include another version of the meat and potatoes menu. One of the better known public Amish foods includes "Shoofly Pie", which was probably first created by German immigrants from Europe. Shoofly pie is a staple that can be served for any meal including breakfast. Essentially it is a pie with a molasses-type filling and obtained its name when pies used to be left on a window ledge to cool and the cook would literally "shoo the flies off of them".

Other Customs

Amish social life and the secretive process of courtship and marriage draws much public curiosity. Consequently there is also a great deal of misinformation and falsehood about the process. One very popular but false notion is that when an Amish man has a daughter of marriageable age he paints his fence blue to advertise the fact. The mixture of untruths and clamor of commercialism is similarly responsible for the confusion regarding the artistic "hex-signs", usually consisting of a six-pointed star, which decorate many buildings in Lancaster County. It may be true that their use was thought of as magical by Swiss Germans who migrated to Lancaster, but there is no connection whatsoever between hex-signs and Amish beliefs (Smith, 1965). It is also believed that an open buggy is used exclusively by young Amish men for courtship purposes while the covered buggy is a family vehicle. Observation will show that this distinction is no longer valid. Buggy shapes and structures, in fact, are often determined by the local *Ordnung*.

While Amish customs may seem to the outsider as quaint in many ways, members of this cultural minority are very much "ordinary folks", just as is any other group of humans. A grandmother confided to one of the authors that though she was not supposed to do so, she was so curious to know who was courting her daughter that on one Saturday night she pushed the living room door open a crack and peeked in. Years later when she revealed this to her daughter and son-in-law they thought her concern was both humorous and understandable.

Amish leaders in Pennsylvania estimate that about eighty percent of their young people remain in the Old Order on attaining adulthood and even with a twenty percent loss the Amish are still among the fastest growing cultural/religious groups in America. This may be attributed to the large families which Amish have; they regard children as "an heritage of the Lord" and the larger the family the more blessed they are of God. Still the trend to leave the community is real; for example, one Lancaster County Amish family had four children, three sons and one daughter. Only the daughter and her husband remained with the Old Order; one son joined with the Beachy Amish, one with the Mennonite Church and the other claimed no church affiliation.

Death, among the Amish, is viewed as part of the natural rhythm of life; it is conceptualized within a religious context based on the biblical principles of the temporality of life. In the same way that the community cares for its mentally or physically handicapped, its aged, and its children and adults in need, it also nurtures the surviving family of the deceased through their time of difficulty. Extra visitation, the bringing of food, and the providing of much care are the ways in which those who have lost loved ones are brought back into full participation in the community. The extra nurture will often go on for a full year after a death (Bryer, 1979). In one of the most emotionally-crucial aspects of life, the Amish reveal a most effective functionalism. It may not be a lifestyle that everyone can appreciate or adopt, but it offers meaning to many of its adherents. in conversation about being Amish with her Amish friend, Susie, Louise Stoltzfus (1994), who grew up Amish quotes her friend as saying,

> As you know, the Amish are not perfect. All the elements of life which are morally wrong are present in our society. We are not free of any human problem. Then Susie's voice changes and she looks full into my eyes. It is her abiding personal faith in the central truths of Amish understandings which hold her life together. . . . "I like being Amish,"she says (42).

References

Aurand, A. Monroe Jr. (1938). *Little Known facts About Bundling in The New World.* Lancaster, PA: The Aurand Press.

Beachy, E. R. (1992). *The Plain People: Tales and Truths About Amish Life.* Harrisburg, PA: Stackpole Books.

Bender, Sue. (1995). *Plain and Simple: A Woman's Journey to the Amish.* San Francisco, CA: HarperSanFrancisco.

Byler, Emma. (1991). *Plain and Happy Living: Amish Recipes and Remedies.* Cleveland, OH: Goosefoot Acres Press.

Bryer, Kathleen N. (1979). The Amish Way of Death. *American Psychologist,* March, 34: 255–261.

Cart, Pauline, ed. (1988). *Over One Hundred of Grandma's Home Remedies.* Millersburg, OH: SMW Cards.

Denlinger, A. Martha. (1981). *Real People: Amish and Mennonites in Lancaster County, Pennsylvania.* Scottdale, PA: Herald Press.

Dyck, Cornelius J., ed. (1967). *An Introduction to Mennonite History: A Popular History of the Anabaptists and the Mennonites.* Scottdale, PA: Herald Press.

Fretz, J. Winfield. (1989). *The Waterloo Mennonites: A Community in Paradox.* Waterloo, ON: Published for the Wilfred Laurier Press for Conrad Grebel College.

Good, Merle & Phyllis Good. (1979). *20 Most Asked Questions About the Amish and Mennonites.* Lancaster, PA: Good Books.

Friesen, John W. (1983). *Schools With A Purpose.* Calgary, AB: Detselig Enterprises.

Harder, M. S. (1949). The Origin, Philosophy, and Development of Education Among the Mennonites. Unpublished Doctoral Dissertation. Los Angeles, CA: The University of Southern California.

Herschberger, Alma. (1992). *Amish Women.* Kalona, IA: Round Table, Inc.

Hostetler, John A. (1974). *Hutterite Society.* Baltimore, MD: The Johns Hopkins University Press.

Hostetler, John A. (1977). *Amish Life.* Scottdale, PA: Herald Press.

Hostetler, John A. (1993). *Amish Society.* fourth edition. Baltimore, MD: The Johns Hopkins Press.

Hostetler, John A. and Gertrude Enders Huntington (1971). *Children in Amish Society: Socialization and Community Education.* New York: Holt, Rinehart and Winston.

Keim, Albert N. (1975). A Chronology of Amish Court Cases. *Compulsory Education and the Amish: The Right Not to be Modern.* Alberta N. Keim, ed. Boston: Beacon Press, 1–15.

Kline, David. (1990). *Great Possessions: An Amish Farmer's Journal.* San Franciso, CA: North Point Press.

Kraybill, Donald B. (1990a). *The Puzzles of Amish Life.* Intercourse, PA: Good Books.

Kraybill, Donald B. (1990b). *The Riddle of Amish Culture.* Baltimore, MD: The Johns Hopkins University Press.

Kraybill, Donald B. and Steven M. Nolt. (1995). *Amish Enterprise: From Plows to Profits.* Baltimore: The Johns Hopkins University Press.

Lehman, Elton. (1994). Providing Healthcare in Amish Country. *Multicultural Education Journal,* 12:2, 11–15.

Minutes of Old Order Amish Steering Committee from October 24, 1973 to October 22, 1980. Second Volume. Gordonville, PA: Gordonville Print Shop.

Nolt, Stephen M. (1992). *A History of the Amish.* Intercourse, PA: Good Books.

Oyer, John S. and Robert S. Kreider. (1989). *Mirror of the Martyrs: Stories of Courage, Inspiringly Retold, of 16th Century Anabaptists Who Gave Their Lives for Their Faith.* Intercourse, PA: Good Books.

Pellman, Rachel T. and Joanne Ranck. (1981). *Quilts Among the Plain People.* Intercourse, PA: Good Books.

Randle, Bill. (1992). Amish Women and Their Kitchens. *Amish Roots: A Treasury of History, Wisdom, and Lord.* John A. Hostetler, ed. Baltimore, MD: The Johns Hopkins University Press, 101–102.

Reimer, Gustav E. and G. R. Gaeddert. (1956). *Exiled by the Czar: Cornelius Jansen and the Great Mennonite Migration, 1874.* Newton, KS: Mennonite Publication House.

Ruth, John L. (1975). *Conrad Grebel: Son of Zurich.* Scottdale, PA: Herald Press.

Schreiber, William I. (1990). *Our Amish Neighbors.* Wooster, OH: The College of Wooster.

Scott, Stephen. (1981). *Plain Buggies: Amish, Mennonites, and Brethren Horse-Drawn Transportation.* Intercourse, PA: Good Books.

Scott, Stephen. (1986). *Why Do They Dress That Way?* Intercourse, PA: Good Books.

Scott, Stephen. (1988). *The Amish Wedding and Other Special Occasions of the Old Order Communities.* Intercourse, PA: Good Books.

Scott, Stephen and Kenneth Pellman. (1990). *Living Without Electricity.* Intercourse, PA: Good Books.

Smith, Elmer L. (1965). *Hex Signs and Other Barn Decorations.* Lebanon, PA: Applied Arts Publishers.

Smith, Elmer L. (1974). *Bundling: A Curious Courtship Custom.* Lebanon, PA: Applied Arts Publishers.

Smith, Elmer L. (1976). *Pennsylvania Dutch Folklore.* Lebanon, PA: Applied Arts Publishers.

Smith, Elmer L. (1979). *Meet the Mennonites in Pennsylvania Dutchland.* Lebanon, PA: Applied Arts Publishers.

Smith, C. Henry. (1957). *The Story of the Mennonites.* Fourth edition. Newton, KS: Mennonite Publication Office

Stoltzfus, Louise. (1994). *Amish Women: Lives and Stories.* Intercourse, PA: Good Books.

Toews, John A. (1975). *A History of the Mennonite Brethren Church: Pilgrims and Pioneers.* Fresno, CA: Board of Christian Literature, General Conference of Mennonite Brethren Churches.

Warner, James A and Donald M. Denlinger. (1969). *The Gentle People.* n.p.: Galahad Books.

Wenger, J. C. (1966). *The Mennonite Church in America.* Scottdale, PA: Herald Press.

Yoder, Elmer S. (1987). *The Beachy Amish Mennonite Fellowship Churches.* Hartville, OH: Diakonia Ministries.

Yoder, Elmer S. (1990). *I Saw It in THE BUDGET.* Hartville, OH: Diakonia Ministries.

Zielinski, John M. (1975). *The Amish: A Pioneer Heritage.* Des Moines, IA: Wallace Homestead Book Co.

Zook, Lee J. (1993). Slow-moving Vehicles. *The Amish and The State.* Donald B. Kraybill, ed. Baltimore, MD: The Johns Hopkins University Press, 145–162.

Chapter 3

Perceptions of Amish in Literature

Introduction

"Journalists and visitors in general, tend to romanticize the Amish as an enchanting paradise, breathlessly idyllic, until inconsistencies are discovered" (Good, 1985, 10).

Whenever we read about cultures other than our own we tend to evaluate unusual customs or beliefs from the standpoint of our own lifestyle; after all, it's only natural. Being involved in a situation where significant cultural differences are obvious and impinge on one's personal life-space, can on occasion cause cultural shock (Friesen, 1993). When the apparent cultural differences are quite pleasant or innocuous, a series of attitudes may be adopted. Sometimes outsiders are simply curious about apparent differences and unique customs. This often happens in the case if the Amish where the tendency is to romanticize the way they live. Literature about the Amish, encountered by tourists, for example—brochures and the like—tend to be very "cute-sy" using words like country living, homey, pastoral, rustic, cozy, wholesome and intimate. Consider this made-for-the-tourist description a barn-raising:

> Josie Miller lowers his head for a few moments of prayer. His two main concerns today are that no one gets hurt during the barn-raising and that each mortise and tenon (joints) fit together correctly. . . . Today there will be 500 Amish and Mennonite workers laboring on this barn as volunteers. . . . Each will have an assignment. Any one of them could make a mistake and hurt himself or someone else. Building a barn in one day can be very stressful for everyone. . . ."Teamwork is everything", he tells them, speaking in Pennsylvania Dutch, their German dialect—push-pull, heave and hoist, all at the right time, in the right direction. . . . As he watches them disappear into the cold early evening, Josie Miller nods and smiles. His morning prayer has been answered (Randolph, 1993, 8–10).

Tourists, of course, are entitled to a certain amount of romanticism; after all, to participate in light-hearted, fun experiences is one of the objectives of touring. The difficulty with this kind of approach, however, is that when one actually comes face-to-face with someone of another cultural background the conversation is often stilted and overshadowed by an uninformed, patronizing attitude of ethnocentrism. In the case of the Amish, the literature is often to blame for promoting this kind of slant, reflecting as it does a kind of glamorous and adventuresome yet shallow orientation.

There are two extremes often indulged in by cultural observers; first, ethnocentrism, that is, the belief that one's cultural perspective is immeasurably superior to any other; and second, cultural relativity, which is the idea that a culture must be evaluated according to its own standards, and those alone (Haviland, 1990). Following this orientation, one should be able to develop the ability to view the beliefs and customs of other people within the context of their culture rather than one's own (Bates and Plog, 1990). The fundamental underlying beliefs of cultural relativism include the notion that every culture or society has its own coherence, integrity and logic. All cultural configurations are equally valid as variations of the human experience. Those who hold this view believe that all persons are to some extent culturally-bound because culture provides the individual with some sense of identity—something to believe in, to hold onto. When this "bond with society" grows *too* strong, ethnocentrism results. It manifests itself in a spirit of cultural self-centredness, the tendency to judge other societies by the standards of one's own. It is by no means a phenomenon exclusive to western societies; it is a common human reaction to diversity (Bates and Plog, 1990).

Most observers of Amish society are hardly bothered by the vibes of ethnocentrism, though they might be accused of it, and they completely avoid the cultural relativist mode. After all, if the idea is to avoid "the world" as much as possible, how could another lifestyle possibly have any form of spiritual validity? Most visitors to Amish country are too impressed with Amish appearances of old fashioned, country style living to bother with any notion of cultural ethnocentrism or relativity. To be fair, who does not develop romantic feelings when viewing a picture of a horse-drawn sleigh being pulled across a snow-laden country lane backed by a row of traditional-style Pennsylvania or Ohio houses with candle-lit windows decked with lace curtains? For the most part the Amish are not viewed by tourists as people; they are simply seen as prototypes of a country fantasy. Their way of life is *so* beautiful, *so* peaceful, *so* idyllic—*so* unreal!

Need for Authenticity

Several years ago, during a conversation of one of the authors with an enterprising young Hutterite writer-turned-publisher (Hofer, 1991), it became obvious that books being published by the firm he was representing reported only "the good things" about his community. When confronted about this stance, the young writer immediately pleaded guilty to the charge, claiming that if he "told the whole truth he would never be welcomed back by his people—even for a visit".

Hofer's book is a collection of folksy stories about growing up Hutterite. He appears to do little fictionalizing in these stories, and even indulges in elaborating a few of the more "dangerous incidents" which might portray Hutterites in a bad light to the outside world. For example, he tells about the time when the "colony boys" put some home-grown marijuana in the women's tea and then describes how they all felt so "good" after drinking it. He also shares a story about hot-wiring a truck and then using it to sneak off to the local movie house to see the film, "Uncle Buck". Hofer warns his readers that his stories "might" be fictional, but readers can judge for themselves. Few of his readers likely possess enough knowledge about Hutterite ways to be able to make a personal judgment. It must be noted, however, that Hofer's "bad image" stories are all about the antics of *unbaptized* youth and should therefore not be charged against the moral account of the overall colony.

Hofer is not the only Anabaptist writer to tell "less than the whole truth" in writing about his background. In fact, this tendency is fairly widespread among authors whose backgrounds represent closed or folk societies other than Anabaptists. These groups usually have severe restrictions about what can be said or written about them. In effect this constitutes another effective form of social control. A corollary purpose of this tack may be to persuade outsiders to believe that the lifestyles of the closed group is superior, more "spiritual" perhaps, than that of members of the dominant society. In Amish literature the result is that the people are portrayed in a bit better, but quite unrealistic light than might be the case. Hofer also admitted that since he left the colony *before* he was baptized he is always welcome to visit and his family has hopes that someday he will be repentant and return to the colony permanently. Still he guards very carefully the nature of his observations as though to assure himself that the door will always be open should he decide to return to colony life.

"Tell it not in Gath"

The Anabaptist penchant for "telling only positive tales at school" has an ancient historical base in the biblical account of an incident in the history of the tribe of Israel when they tried to keep the story of King Saul's cause of death from enemy Philistine ears. King Saul was their *first* king, and although he did not completely fulfill their expectations as a monarch, the Jewish Nation was very concerned that any news about his inappropriate behavior in committing suicide should not reach the ears of their enemies, the Philistines. Therefore, the warning:

> Tell it not in Gath, proclaim it not in the streets of Ashkelon, lest the daughters
> of the Philistines be glad, lest the daughters of the uncircumcised rejoice
> (2 Samuel 1:20 NIV).

Anabaptists, it seems, and perhaps ethnocultural communities generally, do not like to have their histories portrayed with any shading of negativity. Early Mennonite writers, in fact, were sometimes thought of as "liars and rascals" by their more conservative members who felt that even the act writing about their life-style was wrong and sinful (Hofer, 1991, 3). Some observers have noted that early American Anabaptist writers chose to emphasize a positive-only perspective because they were motivated by the difficulties they experienced in terms of trying to attain a positive public image when they first migrated to North America (Palmer, 1972; Friesen, 1977). Therefore, as a means of promoting such, only the praiseworthy aspects of their histories are told.

A contemporary Mennonite writer, Rudy Wiebe, recently retired from the Department of English at The University of Alberta, twice suffered the blows of criticism and ostracism from his Mennonite community. Initially, he was ostracized when he published *Peace Shall Destroy Many*, a candid story about growing up in a Mennonite community (Wiebe, 1962), and, more recently, when he wrote *My Lovely Enemy* (Wiebe, 1983). In this book Wiebe relates the sordid story of a love affair between a Mennonite professor and his graduate student. Wiebe was fired as editor of the *Mennonite Brethren Herald* because of the critical castigation which his first book levelled at his home community, and when his second novel was reviewed in the same publication, the then editor was severely criticized for doing so. That editor later also resigned, although he cited personal reasons for his action.

In a co-authored book written about Orthodox Doukhobors, some years ago, the authors were urged to tell only the "good things" about the Doukhobors since the bad things had already been written up by other authors (Friesen and Verigin, 1989). The Doukhobors are a Russian-born pacifist group who were neighbors to the Mennonites during their sojourn in that country. The Doukhobors migrated to Canada in 1899. A militant subsect of the Doukhobors, the Sons of Freedom, have garnered most of the press on behalf of the Doukhobors even though they comprise a very small portion of the total population. Among their most notorious deeds has been the practice of burning buildings, both public and private, as a means of protesting materialism. Current estimates are that there are only about 50 adherents to the Sons of Freedom movement, but they garner about 95 percent of the publicity about the sect (Schmidt, 1986). Against this background one can understand why adhering Doukhobors would prefer that "only the good things" be told about them.

Amish Portrayals

A cursory examination of the more popular literature about Amish people will render a similar impression to that outlined above. This appears particularly so when their lifestyle is characterized by Mennonite writers. Unfortunately there are very few Amish writers with which one can make comparisons. The bulk of the literature analyzed here appears to be targeted at tourists for the implicit purpose of explaining Amish life to outsiders. Some illustrative examples will substantiate this hypothesis.

American Beginnings

When one first undertakes an investigation of most Anabaptist writings about their history, some very positive-sounding titles emerge, for example, *But Not Forsaken* (Brenneman, 1957); *Exiled by the Czar: Cornelius Jansen and the Great Mennonite Migration* (Reimer and Gaeddert, 1956); *They Seek a Country: A Survey of Mennonite Migrations With*

Special Reference to Kansas and Gnadenau (Wiebe, 1959); *Mennonite Country Boy: The Early Years of C. Henry Smith* (Smith, 1962); *Mennonite Exodus: The Rescue and Resettlement of the Russian Mennonites Since the Communist Revolution* (Epp, 1966); *Lost Fatherland: The Story of the Mennonite Emigration from Soviet Russia, 1921–1927* (Toews, 1967); *Adventures in Faith: The Background in Europe and the Development in Canada of the Bergthaler Mennonite Church of Manitoba* (Gerbrandt, 1970); *Call to Faithfulness: Essays in Mennonite Studies* (Poettcker and Regehr, 1972); *Open Doors: The History of the General Conference Mennonite Church* (Pannabecker, 1975); *Banished for Faith* (Waltner, 1979); *One Quilt, Many Pieces* (Reimer, 1983); and *Living with Conviction: The Memoirs of Siegfried Bartel* (Bartel, 1994).

The history of the initial Amish sojourn on this continent reflect a similar stance: for example, *The Gentle People* (Warner and Denlinger, 1969); *The Quiet Land* (Warner, 1970). *The Amish: A Pioneer Heritage* (Zielinski, 1975); *Real People: Amish and Mennonites in Lancaster County,* (Denlinger, 1981); *A Quiet and Peaceable Life* (Ruth, 1985); *This is Good Country* (Clark, 1988); and, *Our Amish Neighbors* (Schreiber, 1990). Amish origins are described in warm, glowing terms, vividly portraying the concepts of peace, tranquility, unity and community. For example:

> They are a culture born out of turbulent times when the Christian world was dividing into liberal and conservative factions. They are God-fearing people who believe in following the teachings of the Bible. They live simple and somewhat uncomplicated lives because they feel God commands this of them. They are simply a people who are following the dictates of their consciences (Kult, 1986, 4).

> Stemming from the conservative Old Order Amish are many more liberal sects, each with its own varied forms of customs and worship. Despite the differences, however, all are bound together by their traditions, basic beliefs and code of ethics. Their ideal is to live simple, work-filled lives, with humility and obedience to the word of God (Warner, 1970, ix).

> . . . another unity that the Amish have preserved is that of work and pleasure. The lives of fellow creatures and our delight in those lives are great possessions. And these are secured and made available by great possessions that are cultural. . . . [the Amish] look at the world and find it good, and . . . they honor its goodness in their daily work . . . (Berry, 1990, xii–xiii).

> . . . to this day there are no books printed that can fully explain the true spiritual, brotherly love of their religious faith. There are no words found in any language that can explain the basic fundamentals of their faith that was inherited from ancestors of many generations ago, which was granted to them through the grace of our Lord Jesus Christ, and to this day cultivated as their every day mission (Fisher, 1978, 370).

Bathed in these genteel terms, the Amish have justifiably been idolized by people from other, less historically-blessed social sectors. During the Vietnam War era, for example, the Amish became the "symbol of the simple lifestyle which many young people who rejected militarism and materialism idealized " (Clark, 1988, 164). Their effective control of outside cultural influences has been envied by many North Americans weary of resisting the pressures of a technologically-driven, pleasure-seeking society. To an extent, the Amish have created a distinct counterculture rooted in Christian understanding. Their intent has been to combat assimilation by creating a system for living which "allows little deviation and extends to virtually every daily aspect of life" (Scott, 1986, 22). Due in part to the nature of the literature describing their way of life, however, the attention of observers has been drawn to the uniqueness of Amish ways without any awareness of the intrinsic press for conformity or the individual struggles emanating therefrom.

Amish Philosophy

The Amish philosophy or way of looking at life is quite specific, much of it based on an oral tradition explicated for the neonate by elders and parents. Deviancy is quickly attended to and, hopefully, corrected, the transgressor being made well aware of the serious nature of the errant act. Contrast this reality with the descriptions encountered by the tourist:

> Tara and I took a seat among the tomato plants and corn stalks and silently watched as these flowers unfolded. The beauty of the flowers made me appreciate even more the beauty of those with whom I was sharing them . . . the beauty of the Amish (Kult, 1986, 50).

> Practices that identify the Amish as a people draw them together and accentuate their differences from mainstream culture. Accepted ways . . . all build parameters that help the Amish to live humbly, gently and peacefully with God's people and earth (Seitz, 1991, 9).

> I had an obsession with the Amish. Plain and simple. Objectively it made no sense. I, who worked hard at being special, fell in love with a people who valued being ordinary. . . . I didn't know when I first looked at an Amish quilt and felt my heart pounding that my soul was starving, that an inner voice was trying to make sense of my life (Bender, 1995, xi–xii).

The Amish must be viewed as a socio-religious group with attending economic stipulations of a very strict variety. For the past three centuries they have tried to maintain a rather close relationship between religious beliefs and the everyday activities of their members (Smith, 1978, 5). This admixture has necessitated the formation of a close link between daily behavior and earning a living. It also has historical roots for the Amish, as Glick (n.d.) puts it," . . . being ethnically Swiss, they have a pronounced need for sharing and group involvement. A loner is a rare thing among these people. They just naturally like to do things together."

This sense of "comprehensive" community distinguishes the Amish from the workings of dominant society. It is a difficult orientation for outsiders to comprehend. For example, and in more poetic terms:

. . . the academic world and science are preoccupied with theory and the reconstruction of the order of nature while the an Amish person is simply awed by the orderliness of the seasons, the heavens, the world of growing plants, the animals, and the process of living and dying, The Amish, with this philosophy, have prospered on the land more often than their English neighbors who are engulfed in the high cost of mechanization and finally forced to sell and move to industrial or more lucrative livelihoods (Warner and Denlinger, 1969, 132).

Clearly a sense of being superior is evident in the comparison of the Amish lifestyle with that of their "English " neighbors. In addition, we are led to believe that

The Amish community experiences little delinquency in minors, causes and fights no wars, uses no polluting machines, eschews materialism, and has no economically-based class system (Arons, 1976, 134).

In addition:

The latest discoveries of science and the most recent inventions of electricity, tractor, and automobile have not penetrated the lives of the Amish; nevertheless, the restless, curious, and acquisitive advocate of gadgets of fashion, mechanics, and science may find here a healthy antidote (Schreiber, 1990, 6).

and,

Because of their frugality and self-sufficiency, they are in many ways insulated from the crises which so often disrupt modern society (Byler, 1991, iv).

Finally:

Their generous brotherhoods. . . are made up of hard-working and generally prosperous people. Their neighborliness, self-control, goodwill and thrift contribute immeasurably to the foundations of our civilization . . . candidates for the Biblical way of life which nonresistant Christians alone can fulfill are altogether too few (Hostetler, 1975, 37).

In sociological terms, there is a price to pay for these virtues. That price includes implicit obedience to order of the community, respect for and adherence to religious discipline and unquestioning conformity. Rugged individualism is a non-entity in Amish society. The regulations governing their daily lives are in effect from early childhood through adulthood. Even the arena of child play is not exempt. For example:

. . . one school has forbidden the use of baseball gloves and hard balls at school. By the children's playing with a sponge ball or other soft ball, and no gloves, baseball does not become a competitive game with worldly methods which might range out of control among teenagers and be carried on into adulthood (Fisher and Stahl, 1986, 9).

School rules include:

1. Come in when the bell rings and quiet down immediately.
2. Do not leave school grounds without permission.
3. Do not take any school property without permission.
4. Do not play in or around toilets. . . .
6. Do not write on books or any school property. . . .
8. Do not use bad or unclean language. . . .
9. Do not copy, cheat or lie.
10. Help with the singing. . . .
12. Be truthful, honest, and respectful, *always* (Hostetler and Huntington, 1992, 88).

Figure 3-1. Extended family living—Amish style.

In return for playing by the rules, the Amish member receives a durable identity, a sense of belonging to a distinctive people, a meaningful world view, a keen sense of social roots and an unwavering emotional security (Kraybill, 1990, 108–109). Add to this the experience of being misunderstood by many members of the public and a fairly normal set of juxtaposed opposites—love-hate, joy-peace, happy-unhappy, and the like, enable the Amish to join the rest of the human family as bonafide members.

Amish Lifestyle

There is considerable truth to the statement that much of the Amish way of life resembles the way most Americans lived a century ago (Scott, 1988; Scott and Pellman, 1990). Perhaps public admiration for their way of doing things simply represents a nostalgic yearning for the "good old days" in which such virtues as hard-work, hospitality and neighborliness allegedly abounded. For example:

> There is a variously-told story of a plain-dressed Dunkard accosted on the streets of a Pennsylvania town by an evangelical young man who asked, "Brother, are you saved?'" The long-bearded Dunkard did not respond immediately. He pulled out a piece of paper and wrote on it, then handed it to the stranger. "Here," he said, "are the names and addresses of my family, neighbors and people I do business with. Ask them if they think I'm saved. I could tell you anything" (Ruth, 1985, 62).

If one listens carefully to those who speak longingly of the "good old days," this kind of religious testimony would have fit almost any rural sectors of North American life a century ago. The same may be said for this observation:

> I have seen many a modern farmer so busy in his field that he barely had time to wave. But, every Amish farmer working his land with his team of horses always had time to stop by the fence for a chat (Zielinski, 1975, 14).

Also:

> The elderly are highly respected in Amish society. Older persons do everything they can to help the young get started. But the young respect their parents and grandparents and involve them in meaningful ways of being useful. The grandparents gleaning after the harvest . . . etch a parable of Amish life (Good, 1985, 124).

and,

> "The land is God's," Eli said. "It's my job and the job of every Amish person to take care of it for him. We mustn't try to change or conquer nature or exploit the land. That would be going against God's way. When Eli talked about the land, he was happy (Bender, 1995, 63).

For the most part the Amish probably do not "play to their audience," but are concerned with the careful protection and nurture of their children in an effort to maintain cultural continuity and cultural integrity and to remain a discrete minority steadfast to their own vision of the good life (Hostetler and Huntington, 1971, 116; Keim, 1976). Their methodology naturally involves community discipline as well as community support, but only the latter appears to be highlighted in "touristic" presentations to the general public.

Reading Between the Lines

The poetic and unrealistic image of the Amish probably contributes to feelings of envy and inadequacy on the part of some casual observers. Imagine contrasting one's own harried middle-class urban lifestyle, with all of its self-imposed demands and responsibilities with that of the pastoral, peaceful "people of God":

> I remember many nights arriving home past midnight and lying on the grass watching the stars dance in the sky. It would be quiet and peaceful, and I felt as if I just might be in touch with God. To me, this is what being Amish is all about (Kult, 1986, 5).

As the biblical account will attest, all people of God have their human side, including the Jewish patriarchs: Abraham, Isaac, Jacob, David, Peter and Paul. As members of Christendom believe, these individuals and their corresponding families or communities, were "in touch with God" in the same sense that the Amish and members of other forms of structured Christian communities may be in touch with God. However,

> As it often happens when people attempt to be as Christ-like, consistent and perfect as possible, several results surface again and again. . . . the dual themes of perfection and humility provide fertile milieu for many, but tear other persons apart. . . . those who can't stand the tension suffer emotional and spiritual anguish (Good and Good, 1979, 76).

> The quest for peace with God is sometimes advertised as the simple process of seeking and finding. However, after the initial experience the concomitant community produces guidelines consisting of rewards, punishments, sanctions and taboos by which that process is to be continued. In the case of the Amish, they also believe that if anything is a hindrance to the spiritual well-being of the church it should be abstained from (Scott, 1981, 4).

These hidden directives may not be immediately visible to the outsider but they are certainly well-known to younger members within folk communities like the Amish. A closer look will reveal the extent to which these guidelines apply to the various sectors of "ordinary life." For starters, warnings are given. For example, many plain people see the large-scale putting off of plain clothing as part of the apostasy of the end times, and refer to the biblical prophecy concerning a "great falling away" (Scott, 1986, 12).

Warnings also take on a specificity not immediately apparent to those not familiar with Anabaptist ways. For example:

An Amish youth who quits smoking, or stops telling the usual dirty jokes, or gives up the rowdy barn dances is immediately suspected of fellowship with the Mennonites. Of all the ways youth can rebel, association with the Mennonites or some other religious order is the most feared (Naylor, 1977, 154).

Moving away from the arena of warnings is the matter of informal social control. Even the idyllic world of the Amish quilter is not void of some elements of group protocol and influence—some of it quite restricting for the semi-skilled quilter.

No one wants to be next to the fastest quilter because she will be ready to "roll" before they are. Straight lines are easier to quilt than curves so the less experienced quilters will sit at those places if they exist (Pellman and Ranck, 1981, 16).

Being assigned to the kitchen when you would rather quilt can be humbling. It is sometimes the younger girls whose stitches are not yet tiny enough or neat enough who get that job (Pellman and Ranck, 1981, 18).

Conformity to group expectations is evident even in the recreational aspects of Amish life, and with the "encouragement" of group approval or disapproval one is motivated to quilt faster, be neater and try to make smaller stitches. In addition, forms of approval or non-approval also apply to other constituencies. For example, an Amish woman, in speaking of another Amish group slightly less strict than hers, commented, "They iron too much" (Ruth, 1985, 23).

Closer to home is family life, another arena in which the "human element" of Amish lifestyle becomes apparent. In large families, sibling rivalry is not uncommon, even though it is probably not quite as intense as in dominant society. After many hours of bending over picking strawberries in the hot sun, tempers might occasionally flare. One of the boys will grab a horse whip and chase an innocent victim around the pasture until the offended one gives in, and throwing himself on the ground cries out, "Go ahead and kill me" (Kult, 1986, 36).

The Amish believe that customs are good because they are old and therefore they are authentic or true. How or why the rules came to be in the first place is not important to them; they must be obeyed. Without this requirement there is no certainty of any future with God. The Amish firmly believe that modern civilization will come to a terrible ruin, and only a few have a chance at salvation (Naylor, 1977, 44). Thus the implicit rationale for explicit obedience, whether enforced by coaxing, example or coercion, is the only safe route. The popular Amish literature says little about this, nor does it give much hint of the attending spiritual tension with which every Amish individual must cope.

An Amish Perspective

The Amish child has an enormous sense of security in community. The practice of mutual aid and caring for one another assures children that they will be supported and kept from complete loneliness, "from the time they are born until the day they die" (Fisher and Stahl, 1986, 91).

The Amish provide a social model wherein the individual's needs are fulfilled not through the delights of individualism, but in sacrifice and submission to a greater collective good. There are no promises of free-wheeling self-fulfillment in Amish life, but the individual is cared for and cherished by a supportive social system—a humane and durable promise (Kraybill, 1989, 259).

This assurance is comforting to the individual and the "fleeting pleasures" of the outside world are readily viewed as temporary, risky and even dangerous. In the meanwhile the Amish community offers approved outlets to meet all aspects of the human need—physically, socially, and spiritually. Note these expressions written by an Amish writer describing the view "from the inside," and catch the "human elements" of (i) caring, (ii) loneliness, (iii) hurting, (iv) humor, (v) belonging and (vi) prayer.

(i) *Caring:*

To Susan he [her husband] seemed so strong and capable. His voice was so kind. She hoped she would never disappoint him. He was a quiet person, and so patient (Hochstetler & Hochstetler, 1987, 9).

(ii) *Loneliness:*

No visiting ministers had been through this year. Mart and Susan longed once more to have fellowship with other Amish families. They enjoyed their own Bible reading and singing, but they needed fellowship with others too (Hochstetler & Hochstetler, 1987, 171).

(iii) *Hurting:*

A short while later as they knelt for the evening prayer, their hearts ached for the young widow and the six little children. Only God could heal their broken hearts (Hochstetler & Hochstetler, 1989, 22).

(iv) *Humor:*

Now the bachelor hears some voices, and he stares in disbelief! Surely that can't be! Yes, sure enough, a whole gang of them, giggling, talking women-folk coming straight for his cabin. Too late to run out the front door! If only there was a back door! At the last minute he decides to quick climb the ladder to the loft and escape to the very far corner (Hochstetler & Hochstetler, 1991, 52).

(v) *Belonging:*

They beckoned "Come!" Mart and Susan knew that it would mean leaving family and friends all over again. But they were still young, and the urge to go back to the land they had so loved was great, so great it was almost like a magnet (Hochstetler & Hochstetler, 1989, 146).

(vi) *Prayer:*

She made one last climb to her spot on Olsen Hill to pray and talk with the Heavenly Father before they left. She needed this moment to renew her faith. She didn't know where her special spot would be near her new home, but she knew she'd find one somewhere (Hochstetler & Hochstetler, 1991, 69).

Conclusion

The reality of Amish life is that it is first and foremost a *human* lifestyle, albeit somewhat unique in comparison to that of other ethnocultural communities or that of dominant North American society. We must not, however, be distracted by their atypical lifestyle.

There is a good deal of literature about the Amish that is both informative and descriptive, but, unfortunately, it will not likely be easily encountered by the many tourists (Scott, 1981; Good, 1985; Hostetler, 1975; Hostetler, 1993; Kraybill, 1989; Kraybill, 1990; Schreiber, 1990, and Hostetler and Huntington, 1992). Casual observers of the Amish will likely continue to be influenced by more poetic and mythological renderings, thanks to their perusal of the most easily-accessible materials. The tragedy of this reality is that the Amish will continue to be perceived as a kind of ideal folk society, and their true humanity will not be appreciated. Thus any lessons to be learned from their community may be lost because of the distraction of their unique "cultural covering." This may also restrict any meaningful inter-cultural interaction with members of the "outside world" which could serve to reinforce the mutuality of the human family. Herscheberger (1992) appears to appreciate this when she thanks the participants in her study of Amish women. She concludes her book by expressing the wish that her work will answer many questions about Amish women and "help people to realize that the Amish people are real people too" (3).

References

Arons, Stephen. (1976). Compulsory Education: The Plain People Resist, *Compulsory Education and the Amish: The Right Not to be Modern*. Albert N. Keim, ed. Boston: Beacon Press, 124–135.

Bartel, Siegfried. (1994). *Living with Conviction: The Memoirs of Siegfried Bartel*. Winnipeg, MB: CMBC Publications.

Bates, Daniel G. and Fred Plog. (1990). *Cultural Anthropology*. third edition. New York: McGraw-Hill Publishing Company.

Bender, Sue. (1995). *Plain and Simple: A Woman's Journey to the Amish*. San Francisco, CA: HarperSanFrancisco.

Berry, Wendell. (1990). Foreword. *Great Possessions: An Amish Farmer's Journal*. by David Kline. San Francisco, CA: North Point Press, xi–xiii.

Brenneman, Helen Good. (1957). *But Not Forsaken*. Scottdale, PA: Herald Press.

Byler, Emma. (1991). *Plain & Happy Living: Amish Recipes & Remedies*. Cleveland, OH: Goosefoot Acres Press.

Clark, Allen B. (1988). *This is Good Country: A History of the Amish of Delaware, 1915–1988*. Gordonville, PA: Gordonville Print Shop.

Denlinger, A. Martha. (1981). *Real People: Amish and Mennonites in Lancaster County, Pennsylvania*. Scottdale, PA: Herald Press.

Epp, Frank H. (1966). *Mennonite Exodus: The Rescue and Resettlement of the Russian Mennonites Since the Communist Revolution*. Altona, MB: D. W. Friesen & Sons.

Fisher, Gideon. (1978). *Farm Life and its Changes*. Gordonville, PA: Pequea Publishers.

Fisher, Sara E. and Rachel J. Stahl. (1986). *The Amish School*. People's Place Booklet No. 6. Intercourse, PA: Good Books.

Friesen, John W. (1977). *People, Culture & Learning*. Calgary, AB: Detselig Enterprises.

Friesen, John W. (1983). *Schools With a Purpose*. Calgary, AB: Detselig Enterprises.

Friesen, John W. (1993). *When Cultures Clash: Case Studies in Multiculturalism*. second edition. Calgary, AB: Temeron Books.

Friesen, John W. and Michael L. Verigin. (1989). *The Community Doukhobors: A People in Transition*. Ottawa, ON: Borealis Press.

Gerbrandt, Henry J. (1970). *Adventures in Faith: The Background in Europe and the Development in Canada of the Bergthaler Mennonite Church of Manitoba*. Altona, MB: D. W. Friesen and Sons Ltd.

Glick, Daniel M. (n.d.). *The Amish of Lancaster County*. A Brochure. Smoketown, PA: Mennonite Tour Guide.

Good, Merle. (1985). *Who are the Amish?* Intercourse, PA: Good Books.

Good, Merle and Phyllis Good. (1979). *20 Most Asked Questions About the Amish and the Mennonites*. People's Place Booklet No. 1. Intercourse, PA: Good Books.

Haviland, William A. (1990). *Cultural Anthropology*. sixth edition. Fort Worth, TX: Holt, Rinehart and Winston.

Herschberger, Alma. (1992). *Amish Women*. Kalona, IA: Round Table, Inc.

Hochstetler, Martin and Susan Hochstetler. (1987). *Life On The Edge of The Wilderness*. Coalgate, OK: Published by the authors.

Hochstetler, Martin and Susan Hochstetler. (1989). *Farm Life in the Hills*. Coalgate, OK: Published by the authors.

Hochstetler, Martin and Susan Hochstetler. (1991). *Cabin Life on the Koonenai*. West Union, OH: Published by the authors.

Hofer, Samuel. (1991). *Born Hutterite*. Saskatoon, SK: Hofer Publishing.

Horst, Mel. (1959). *Among the Amish*. Lebanon, PA: Applied Arts Publishers.

Hostetler, John A. (1975). *Amish life*. Scottdale, PA: Herald Press.

Hostetler, John A. (1993). *Amish Society,* fourth edition. Baltimore, MD: The Johns Hopkins Press.

Hostetler, John A. and Gertrude Enders Huntington. (1971). *Children in Amish Society: Socialization and Community Education.* New York: Holt, Rinehart and Winston.

Hostetler, John A. and Gertrude Enders Huntington. (1992). *Amish Children: Education in the Family, School, and Community.* second edition. Fort Worth, TX: Harcourt Brace Jovanovich College Publishers.

Keim, Albert N., ed. (1976). *Compulsory Education and the Amish: The Right Not to be Modern.* Boston: Beacon Press.

Kraybill, Donald B. (1989). *The Riddle of Amish Culture.* Baltimore, MD: The Johns Hopkins University Press.

Kraybill, Donald B. (1990). *The Puzzles of Amish Life.* People's Place Booklet No. 10. Intercourse, PA: Good Books.

Kult, Phyllis Kathryn. (1986). *Through My Eyes: the Amish Way.* Dover, OH: Newhouse Printing.

Naylor, Phyllis Reynolds. (1977). *An Amish Family.* New York: Lamplight Publishing Co.

Palmer, Howard. (1972). *Land of the Second Chance.* Lethbridge, AB: The Lethbridge Herald.

Pannabecker, Samuel Floyd. (1975). *Open Doors: The History of the General Conference Mennonite Church.* Newton, KS: Faith and Life Press.

Pellman, Rachel T. and Joanne Ranck. (1981). *Quilts Among the Plain People.* People's Place Booklet No. 4. Intercourse, PA: Good Books.

Poettcker, Henry and Rudy A. Regehr, eds. (1972). *Call to Faithfulness: Essays in Mennonite Studies.* Winnipeg, MB: Canadian Mennonite Bible College.

Randolph, John L. (1993). Barn Raising. *Holmes County Traveler,* 5:3, 8–10.

Reimer, Gustav E. and G. R. Gaeddert. (1956). *Exiled by the Czar: Cornelius Jansen and the Great Mennonite Migration, 1874.* Newton, KS: Mennonite Publication Office.

Reimer, Margaret Loewen. (1983). *One Quilt, Many Pieces.* Waterloo, ON: Mennonite Publishing Service.

Ruth, John L. (1985). *A Quiet and Peaceable Life.* People's Place Booklet No 2. Intercourse, PA: Good Books.

Schmidt, Jeremy. (1986). Spirit Wrestlers. *Equinox,* twenty-five, January/February, 60–69.

Schreiber, William I. (1990). *Our Amish Neighbors.* Wooster, OH: The College of Wooster.

Scott, Stephen. (1981). *Plain Buggies: Amish, Mennonite and Brethren Horse-drawn Transportation.* People's Place Booklet No. 3. Intercourse, PA: Good Books.

Scott, Stephen. (1986). *Why Do They Dress That Way?* People's Place Booklet No. 7. Intercourse, PA: Good Books.

Scott, Stephen. (1988). *The Amish Wedding, and Other Special Occasions of Old Order Communities.* People's Place Booklet No. 8. Intercourse, PA: Good Books.

Scott, Stephen and Kenneth Pellman. (1990). *Living Without Electricity.* People's Place Booklet No. 9. Intercourse, PA: Good Books.

Seitz, Ruth Hoover. (1991). *Amish Ways.* Harrisburg, PA: RB Books.

Smith, C. Henry. (1962). *Mennonite Country Boy: The Early Years of C. Henry Smith.* Newton, KS: Faith and Life Press.

Smith, Elmer L. (1978). *The Amish: An Illustrated Essay.* Lebanon, PA: Applied Arts Publishers.

Toews, John B. (1967). *Lost Fatherland: The Story of the Mennonite Emigration from Soviet Russia, 1921–1927.* Scottdale, PA: Herald Press.

Waltner, Emil J. (1979). *Banished for Faith.* Jasper, AR: End-Time Handmaidens, Inc.

Warner, James A. (1970). *The Quiet Land.* Wilmington, DE: The Middle Atlantic Press.

Warner, James A. and Donald M. Denlinger. (1969). *The Gentle People: A Portrait of the Amish.* Lancaster, PA: Stel-mar Publishers.

Wiebe, David V. (1959). *They Seek a Country: A Survey of Mennonite Migrations With Special Reference to Kansas and Gnadenau.* Hillsboro, KS: The Mennonite Brethren Publishing House.

Wiebe, Rudy. (1962). *Peace Shall Destroy Many.* Toronto, ON: McClelland and Stewart.

Wiebe, Rudy. (1983). *My Lovely Enemy.* Toronto, ON: McClelland and Stewart.

Zielinski, John M. (1975). *The Amish: A Pioneer Heritage.* Des Moines, IA: Wallace-Homestead Book Co.

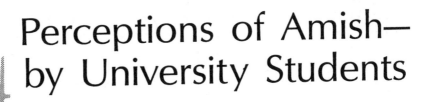

Chapter 4

Perceptions of Amish— by University Students

Most scholars tend to agree with Hostetler's (1993) assessment of the Amish as a folk society, a commonwealth, a sectarian society and a high-context or highly involved-with-one-another culture. Following Durkheim's (Durkheim, 1976; Friesen, 1995) delineation of belief systems as dividing all phenomena into either sacred or profane (secular) domains, the Amish clearly tend towards the former. They perceive all activities, all thoughts, behaviors and institutional structures as having to reflect an attitude of sacredness. Anything not done "for the glory of God" may be considered profane. In consensus with Durkheim's model, the Amish believe that the sacred must be "set apart", and this includes everything in life. They do not believe that any one aspect of life can be separated into individual components. For them *everything* is sacred, and everything must reflect one's duty to God as defined by the *Ordnung* of the community. Naturally this view necessitates adherence to stringent rules when it becomes necessary for the Amish to interact with the outside world. The reins of control get even tighter when some form of contact is required with those individuals who have been excommunicated (banned) by the community.

In the early days of sociology it was held that the normal state for societies was for them to "make progress", not to go downhill. This is sometimes called the steady development theory. Progress was taken for granted, and some even believed it was inevitable (Spencer, 1990). Historian Arnold Toynbee (1946), for example, proposed that all civilizations follow a typical life course and rarely deviate from it. He also suggested that societies sometimes successfully meet a challenge, develop to the "empire" stage and then lose out to the very people they are attempting to serve (or conquer). As a traditional theory, Toynbee's postulations find a ready application to Amish ongoings since it is the objective of their society to "maintain" tradition, rather than "attain" any objective outside of their historical goal. This development is parallel to the work of Ferdinand Tönnies (1988) who postulated that since the time of the Industrial Revolution society generally has evolved from a *Gemeinschaft* (folk or primary) society to a *Gesellschaft* (secondary) society. Applying this theory to the North American scene it would appear that the nation's involvement in war in this century on this continent, would preclude any application of the "steady development" theory. Critics may want to take a long term perspective and argue that in the long haul, that is, over the past two centuries, North American society has indeed grown and "matured", and the total annihilation of the universe is no longer a real threat.

Sorokin (1947) believed that societies generally swing between the two ends of the polarity of "sensate" and "ideational", the former represented by materialistic (sensual) pursuits and the latter stressing ideals or spiritual concerns. Sorokin supported his theory with a longitudinal view of society, suggesting that the Gothic art period was most representative of the sensate orientation and modern society reflects materialistic values.

Earlier than Toynbee, and following the lead of Georg Wilhelm Friedrich Hegel, Marx and Engels identified a recurring process in the history of civilization, viewing social change in the form of a dialectic process. In this model a main idea (thesis) is opposed by an opposite notion (antithesis), and a struggle of ideas ensue. When the dust has settled, a new state or synthesis is born. This new social order then becomes a thesis and is in turn challenged by a new antithesis and the process goes on (Marx and Engels, 1967; Henslin, 1995). Although Marx and Engels applied their theory to the history of human civilization per se, one can detect shadows of its operation in the constant splintering process in Anabaptist history as well. Every major Anabaptist sector—Amish, Hutterites and Mennonites—show ample evidence of this within their ranks.

Secular Views of the Sacred

In an effort to determine the extent to which varying social sectors view the Amish, an informal survey of two groups of university students was conducted in the fall of 1995 with a view to comparing their perceptions of the Amish. One group of students was resident in Ohio Amish country (Holmes, Stark, Wayne Counties) and enrolled in sociology classes at Kent State University, Stark Campus; the other was far removed from the scene, and consisted of a class of students at The University of Calgary in Calgary, Alberta, Canada. None of the Calgary students had every met any Amish individuals. Participants in the study were simply asked to write a paragraph finishing a lead-in sentence, "My impression of Amish is . . . "

The Calgary Sample

The Faculty of Education, Graduate Division of Educational Research, at The University of Calgary has offered an advanced undergraduate course in ethnic studies since 1968. Basically, the course comprises a study of selected case studies of ethnocultural groups including their history and settlement in Canada and subsequent cultural adjustments. Content has featured such communities as Anabaptists (including Amish, Mennonites and Hutterites), Chinese, Doukhobors, French Canadians and Sikhs. For many years the course also incorporated a segment dealing with First Nations, but a parallel survey course on Native education has been made available since 1988.

In the fall of 1995, a class of fifty students in an ethnic studies class were asked to participate in the study. It was evident that they had little knowledge of the Amish; their only class exposure had been to view the film, *The Amish: A People of Preservation.* It is helpful to remember that there *is* an Amish community in Canada, primarily located in Waterloo County, Ontario, and consisting of 17 separate districts. These communities are located about 2,000 miles east of Alberta. After the class had viewed the film they were asked to respond to complete the provided statement. All of them complied with the request. The results of the survey, as expected, indicate a fairly peripheral knowledge of Amish ways mingled with a spirit of romanticism.

We have italicized phrases in each quotation in an attempt to summarize the key intent of each response. We hope that we have been fair to our subjects in doing so. The responses have been recorded in the exact form in which they were returned to the researchers. None of them have been modified in any way.

(i) the Tourist Image

The Amish are a group of people who recognize the true values of what it is to be human. Their values and beliefs bind them to one another during good times and they show the greatest compassion for one another when one is in need. They have tightly-knit family values which I feel the North American lifestyle is lacking. *They are a role model for values that would be nice to restore to present society.*

My impression of Amish is a group of individuals who aren't afraid of practicing their religious beliefs amidst a modern society. They are brave folks who dare to be different in a conformist society. Their simplicity can teach the general public about how chaotic and material-driven our society is. *It makes you wonder who are the crazy ones.*

I feel a sense of "nostalgia" for some strange reason. It is a very simple and loving view of old-fashioned family life, something that is sadly missing from our society today. The youth of today could stand to learn from Amish ways. It certainly wouldn't hurt our youth to participate in some "chores" to keep them out of mischief.

An interesting culture that *lets us look into the way people lived in the past.* They are an honest, hardworking group of individuals where simplicity is prized.

My impression of Amish is that they are a very interesting group. I found it very exciting to watch how one group can survive in today's world yet still maintain a lifestyle from the past. *I would love to go and visit an Amish community and experience first-hand their customs and traditions.* I would also like to witness the close bond all the community members appear to have. I admire the rules (the commandments) that they adhere to and how they cherish them deeply.

Despite these rather general first impressions of Amish life, it should be noted that the attitudes of the students towards the Amish lifestyle portrayed in the film *were* quite positive. In similar fashion, most visitors to Amish country probably conceive of them in a poetic, nostalgic sense; they are viewed as a quiet, peaceful, gentle, country folk who resemble something out of an eighteenth century American furniture catalog.

Some of the responses also conveyed an encouraging element of what might be labelled "emerging tolerance", or "enhanced awareness" about the Amish, that is, the students appeared to have some prior knowledge or insight that enabled them to get past the "tourist" image of other cultures.

(ii) *Towards Cultural Understanding*

My impression of Amish is that they are another group who believe that their culture is the best way to live. Their culture is interesting because although it is very different from ours today. At one time we all lived like they did. Because of this I find it odd that so many people see them as so weird, and go to see them on road trips, etc. *I find their culture interesting because they don't depend on modern technology like we do.* I sometimes think that we depend too much on technology.

My impression is a simplistic kind of people. They have their own values and beliefs that pertain to living. Though I find some of their beliefs different, e.g. youth doing what they please, *I respect their way of living the same as they would respect mine.*

They are people like you and me, who have chosen to live a different lifestyle than the rest of us. I could not live the way they do (maybe I'm a little too materialistic; I need my car and my perfume, etc.). But if they like to live that way, why not? *If it makes them happy, then so be it!*

They are a people who are very devoted to their religious beliefs. Furthermore, they live as they believe and do not feel the need to conform to dominant society. However, I do feel that there is a bit of hypocrisy in their practice of allowing the young people to go out and have fun before they settle down and become baptized. To their disadvantage, the Amish do lose some of the young people who really enjoy this bit of freedom and decide to abandon the community. *Other than this, to each his own, and more power to those who practice what they preach.*

One might expect that a course in ethnic studies would bring out a bit of the "anthropologist" in students' reviews, and this expectation was not disappointing. Several participants attempted to decipher meaning from the fact that the Amish have a strong link to the past but are faced with very challenging conditions as to their future.

(iii) *Analytic*

They are a people who value "simpleness" to the extreme. I see them as having *very* strong ingroup ties that keep their community from being heavily assimilated and thus cause them to be distinct from the rest of society. Myself, being a Mennonite, I understand many of their core beliefs; what I do not understand fully is how they think the old way is *so* important. *I do not see how they understand progress to be in opposition to their faith.* Perhaps if I lived in their villages for a time I might understand this belief more fully.

My impression of Amish is, they tend to live in the past, not wanting to keep up our ever-changing society. In a way, I can admire their distinctiveness and their ability to keep their culture and traditions as well as they have. *Obviously there have been some changes, but they are pretty moderate compared to other cultural groups in our society.*

They do not want to become "slaves of progress" but are finding this to be a difficult task. There does not seem to be an established set of requirements for determining whether or not to accept technology (or certain parts of it), so to us outsiders it appears that there are a lot of inconsistencies. For example, I find it amusing that some Amish farmers will use tractors but take off the rubber tires. It is hard to understand exactly why they don't accept some forms of technology and progress.

The above comments represent the majority of responses, all of them clearly conveying a very positive assessment of Amish life. Naturally, not all of the participants were so influenced nor as enthusiastic as their colleagues. Even with a limited amount of information they took it upon themselves to make pronouncements on Amish life, no doubt reflecting a very public tendency.

(iv) *Making Assessments*

I do not know much about the Amish yet. What I do remember is that the parents of an engaged couple do not know who their daughter is marrying until church on Sunday. It is then announced to the whole congregation, so they find out and at once their marriage procedures begin. *I think that is quite a weird belief and I hope to find out more.*

They are very resilient since they have been able to retain their culture and maintain traditional ways, i.e. using no modern day technology. It is unfortunate that tourists invade their privacy to the extent they do. Hopefully, they will be able to continue their lifestyle, however, *I see this as difficult in a modern society which seemingly values materialism and technology above all things.*

My impression of Amish people is that they are *a culture (religion) that will not persevere* because I don't think they effectively retain their youth and are losing them.

They are a dying breed. They are a culture trying to survive in an industrial world without giving in to mechanism and machinery that they think will corrupt their culture.

The Kent Sample

Students in three sociology classes were asked to respond to the survey question, and a total of one hundred responses were obtained. In reviewing participant responses it soon became evident that geographic proximity has its advantages in terms of being able to procure a wider range of opinions. Even then several of the student responses revealed a fairly unrealistic assessment of Amish ways, probably derived from a basic lack of knowledge of Amish lifestyle. Truly, geographic proximity does not necessarily foster indepth familiarity.

(i) *The Tourist Image*

I respect them very much. I had an Amish nanny when I was little her name was Anna she was wonderful at everything, her cooking, baking, caring of me and my whole family. I used to go to her house on the weekends when my dad would take her home for the weekends. I loved her clothes and she never wore any make-up and she had the most beautiful skin. Her mom and dad worked very hard and had morals that were never broken. I always thought that Amish are the true meaning of family in America. *They are so cute in their beards and bonnets.*

They are people that live in homes with no electricity, don't drive cars, wear plain clothing, the women wear white bonnets and never wear pants, the men wear black hats and suspenders. *They make their living off of selling trail bologna and cheese.* They don't drink alcohol and they drive horse-driven

Figure 4-1. Laundry day—Amish style.

buggies. Their children are raised in all Amish communities and put in all Amish school systems. They must marry within their religion. They make all their own clothes by hand and eat food out of their gardens.

They are a religious group that believes in family unity and God. They do not use our modern day conveniences such as cars, electricity, and running water. *To me the Amish are simple people with a simple purpose, to serve their God.*

My impression of Amish is one of simplicity and a degree of innocence. By this I mean they seem to almost shield themselves from the secular world. I am assuming that it is because of religious beliefs. They must also be people of great inner strength simply because it would be so easy for them to give up and conform to the ways of the world. Sometimes I wonder why they live the way they do. Sometimes I think about how much things they are missing but on the other hand they must be doing something right?

My impression of Amish is that they are very a very self-sufficient people. It is amazing to me the things that they can do without any modern conveniences such as electricity. *I admire that they are able to live and be very productive is such simple ways.*

They have a very simple society. They don't need all the gadgets and futuristic stuff that the rest of society needs. They are proud of who they are and they do not care of society's approval. I think its very interesting how these people live. *Maybe if we adapted some of their ideas, we wouldn't have some of the moral issues to deal with.*

They are very skilled and intelligent people. Some might say their beliefs are out of the ordinary and certainly not modern but I think that not being modern would have benefits. With regard to clothing, for example, their children don't have to worry about the latest fashions thus saving the family money. *By their crafts and homemade foods show they have exceptional abilities.*

They are simple people who do not bother anybody. They do things their own way and keep to themselves.

My impression of Amish is very quiet, docile people. They live in communities that are very simple, but hard to understand. I don't really know to much about them, except I can sometimes tell them apart from others. They seem very proud of their religion. *They have their own beliefs and values and I think that it is great how they stick to their beliefs.*

A number of students were quite sympathetic to Amish ways, and seemed to base their positive impressions and desire to learn on a more subtle form of latent cultural sensitivity.

(ii) *Towards Cultural Understanding*

A group of people who share common religion, values and property. I see Amish as people committed to maintaining a lifestyle that is simple and supportive to family and neighbors. Through a relative who worked at a local children's hospital I met an Amish family and visited their home. *They greeted me warmly, were happy, generous people who appreciated writing letters and sharing news of family. I wish I had more time to write.*

They are hard-working, God-fearing people. Family and religion are important to them and they seem to have a strong sense of moral values. I find their way of life a little bit hypocritical because they don't want technology, yet they use things such as a plow and a horse and buggy (which is still an amount of technology in comparison to cultures before these inventions). *However, I find them relatively friendly, and they don't hurt anyone else, which gives me a good impression of them.*

I respect the Amish for their strict devotion to their religion and beliefs. I grew up in the area and I have been exposed to the Amish and some of their ways. I admire their ability to be able to live and carry on past traditions i.e. horse and buggy, in a society that is ever expanding with technology and growth. *Whenever I see the Amish I am reminded of this past lifestyle and how important it is to get off the roller coaster every once in a while.*

They are very strong, hard working people that believe in what they are doing. *I have much respect for them because I know I would probably go insane if I didn't have my TV or electricity or my car.*

A group of individuals that respect their ancestors and their culture. The Amish are hard workers, and because of that in recent years have benefited substantially economically from "city people". Many that I come into contact with are very wealthy and extremely "in-touch" with society, more than we think.

I respect there work ethic from the ones that I have come to know. I also believe they have a close knit community amongst themselves. *Their way of life is simple and yet they are satisfied with their lives.*

If these student responses are any indication of how Ohio residents generally feel about the Amish, they would seem to indicate that the public has very definite opinions about the internals workings of Amish society and about the degree of interaction that the public might have with the Amish. Projections are also made with regard to the Amish future.

(iii) Analytic

I grew up in Pennsylvania, near Lancaster. We used to go to Amish Country and shop when I was younger. They have their own lifestyle, customs, etc. that are different from the standards of present society. I have met and interacted with some, and they are human beings like the rest of us. They do many things different, but they should be treated with the same attitude as everyone else. They are stereotyped because they are different. I know some German and have interacted with some Amish that way. *They are just the same as us, with the same likes and dislikes..*

My impression of Amish is that theirs is just a different way of life. Granted, it is not one that I would choose for myself. From what I know they are very conservative people who don't believe in taking advantage of modern innovations such as electricity and malls. They seem to be very good cooks. *They also seem to be backwards in their view of female roles.* For example, that women do all cooking, cleaning, and child rearing. I have never heard of a female Amish member occupying any kind of career outside of those areas.

My impression of Amish is hardworking, family-oriented people with a great belief and strength in the way of life they lead. The idea that all they have was given to them by God and no one but he will take that from them. And it is their duty to him to use all they have and flourish from it. *The only tradition or belief I'm not clear on is the practice of shunning? If a person makes a mistake they should be able to be forgiven without their community and family turning against them.*

My impression of Amish is one of respect. I feel that any group of people who can, in this industrial society, flourish primarily off of the land should be admired. Subsequently, I also feel that almost total isolation from your surroundings can be quite *harmful to your groups longevity as a group.*

They are a group of people that seclude themselves from the rest of the world. I *feel that there beliefs have structured their life to a point of complete domination of who they are without allowing room for changing there views based on experience.*

They are a society within a society. They only leave their community when necessary in order to obtain things that they perhaps can't make themselves. Also they appear to be very closed; they do not communicate with others, other than Amish. They are all white persons; I have never seen a Black Amish person. They work the land to survive and are very skilled in so as far as using their hands. They are very religious but I don't know their beliefs as far as male and female roles except that the wives are in the kitchen and the husbands are in the fields.

My impression of the Amish is that they are strict, limiting themselves, backwards in terms of standard of living, separatists, much too controlled by religious beliefs. I don't know any Amish personally though.

The Amish are people of strict moral restraint. This restraint creates a society in which people have no technology. There communities are much closer to each other than is our's. However, *their practice of shunning people, who have failed in some aspect of their society, creates unfair feelings for an individual and fear for an entire community.*

The Amish have been isolated from the rest of Americans if not the world. By choice they live a simple life with not many wants or needs. They have pure and honest beliefs that extend from generation to generation. *Although they shelter themselves from the "outside" world I feel they are beginning to become more "worldly" (If that's possible).*

Contact theory in ethnic studies projects that unless certain conditions are met before, during and after, intercultural contact is made, such experiments can "do more harm than good". The following comments from students would seem to support this theory, if one supposes that Kent University students, who live in Ohio, would have ample opportunity to interact with Amish folk. Contact theory suggests that intercultural contact should include pre-briefing and de-briefing sessions and the contact should be planned and approved by officials from both communities and the participants. In addition, during the time of contact both parties should be mutually engaged in positive, interdependent, non-threatening activities that hold the potential for bonding (Friesen, 1993). Obviously, none of these criteria were in place when the perceptions summed up in the following responses were experienced.

(iv) Making Assessments

Amish help to reinforce the simpler side of life, that I think people in this fast-paced world tend to forget. For example riding in a horse drawn carriage, and not going 65 mph, so slow, and how relaxed. *However, being an outsider I sometimes wonder at the complexities of the Amish people—and wonder if their ideas are misplaced in today's world.*

They are a group of people who live "prehistoric" times. They drive a horse and buggy instead of a car. They do not have electricity or running water. They indulge themselves in none of the "modernized" pleasures such as the movies or frozen microwave dinners, and I hear the girls are "easy" (If you know what I mean).

My impression of Amish is that they are fake. The women act so innocent and like they don't take a bath, but I went out with an Amish girl and she was not very prude at all . . . .They also had a phone and TV.

As a child, I and my family owned a small store in Amish country. We made some really nice friends while being there. I understand some of their reasons and "whys" for their customs and beliefs, but I also have trouble with them. One being—they can't own a vehicle due to Satan being a part of it, yet they ride in vehicles frequently. *I have other problems with their way of life—like their beliefs on shunning, etc.*

They are a not so friendly type of people, they seem to be afraid of the so-called "regular" community. At the same time they seem to be friendly and peaceful. I would like to try to live the way they do. They are good cooks and create good food.

Amish are very strict in their ways. They can be mean and abusive to their wives. They are very conservative when it comes to "outsiders" but when they are around their family and friends or other Amish they are very bold. The children play games just like any other child (e.g. baseball, softball and soccer). *Their children also get in their fair share of trouble.* Of course they cannot get into too much trouble or the others wouldn't be able to talk to them. They represent the traditional family.

They are a very keep to themself society. *I feel that they think they are too good for the rest of us.*

They are very peaceful and quiet people. But I also feel that they miss out on the pleasures in life they can have, because of their religion. *I also think that they somewhat force their children to believe as they do.*

I have grown up in a community with many Amish. They try to make everyone think that they are perfect and do just as the Bible says. They don't believe in a lot of material things and they don't like to make themselves stand out. *But the Amish I know are the biggest gossips you will every meet. They go to church just to spread gossip. They put on good shows.*

They are stubborn because they haven't reformed to the way America is now. They need to make some changes. They are messing up their children. These poor kids get pointed at and made fun of all the time. They should buy a car. *Those buggies are dangerous.*

They are kind and helpful to the people like themselves, but they are suspicious of people unlike themselves *and they often appear cold-hearted and angry because of their uneasiness around those people.*

My impression of Amish is that they're sort of weird. *They need to come together with today's society.* I feel bad for the children who are brought up this way. I suppose that's why so many leave that background.

They are peaceful people. But they are secluded from the rest of the population. I can respect how they live off the land and have a good sense of unity. *But when I visited the Amish country last I felt a sense that they thought they were superior to us regular people, maybe, because they believe they're not as corrupt.* But overall they seem like a nice bunch of people.

My impression of Amish is they are making too much money. Once we bought a puppy off an Amish family, later we went back and bought a second one which was $60 dollars more, we also bought some authentic wood crafts in their shop on the way home I looked at the woodcraft, I think is was a wooden cat; on the bottom it said "made in Mexico". I didn't think their religion allowed them to make such large profits for themselves.

Amishmen are very sexist. My experience with the Amish of Medina and Wayne County Amish people has been that the men treat their wives very poorly. For example, I rarely see them helping her carry packages out of the store or help her into the buggy. I have also found some of them to be dirty. For example, the hem of underskirts (or petticoats). However, that is not my opinion of all Amish, but some of the Amish individuals.

My impression of the Amish is that they are distant and cold emotionally. They are of strong character and morally pure. I also feel they are silly for not taking advantage of the benefits that man has created in innovation and technology.

They take more out of society than they contribute. By establishing restaurants they are making more profit on out secular society than we make off them.

They make their own plain clothes, in which they don't have many and they farm and produce only what they need which is cool. *I like how they are one with nature, but they don't help out by being separate.*

These assessments clearly indicate that even some measure of contact with a particular community does not eradicate the possibility that impressions can be founded on rumor or conjecture.

Ethnicity and Cultural Change

Although theorists who study ethnic change and persistence have varied in their predictions about the future of separatist ethnocultural community life (Driedger, 1989; Fishman, 1989; Elliott & Fleras, 1992), pressures on these communities to conform to the public norm are still a reality. Certainly the potential for ethnicities to disappear altogether is real, but there is also the possibility that modification and selective retention may prolong ethnic identity (Gordon, 1964). In their three centuries of existence the cultural shape of the Amish community and their public image have undergone significant changes. There is little question that the magnitude and severity of public prejudice and discrimination against Amish has probably intensified and a variety of related factors may be identified. The primary reasons for enhanced prejudice against Amish is probably their rapid population increase and enhanced wealth. The higher the population of a group who may be the target of prejudice and discrimination, the higher the intensity or degree of malice towards them (Friesen, 1993).

Possibly, with a few exceptions, immigrant ethnocultural communities who come to North America, tend to assimilate (or minimally, integrate) with mainstream society, partially caused, no doubt by the tendency of succeeding generations to adopt mainstream customs and values with less resistance than that manifested by the first generation of immigrants. The North American standard of living is envied around the world, and the two countries, Canada and the USA, are often described as the most desirable countries within which to live. When one is finally able to obtain residence in such a highly-acclaimed place to live, who can resist the overwhelming, although often implicit, pressures to conform?

Besides the inevitable changes within the Amish community brought about by the forces of assimilation (or internal assessments), there are signs of a gradual transformation of their preference for the traditional acceptance of order to an appreciation for elements of the modern world. Consider, for example, the successes enjoyed by many Amish-run businesses who also find it necessary to utilize some of the modern conveniences of good bookkeeping practices—computers and the like. Amish businessmen may not own a computer, but they are allowed to buy the services of a computer company that will provide them with assessment sheets and the like. The periodic splintering of more conservative groups away from the Old Order has also influenced the Old Order to become more moderate in outlook, making them more willingly adopt "worldly" devices that make their jobs easier. A woodworker's machines may be powered by a gasoline engine, but the devices run by the engine represent a very refined technology capable of producing some very high quality merchandise.

Bennett (1995) argues that the melting-pot theory is slowly being replaced with the concept of cultural pluralism in American thinking. In its purest form, cultural pluralism is a process of compromise characterized by mutual appreciation and respect between two or more ethnic communities. In a pluralist society, members of different groups are permitted to retain many of their cultural and religious ways as long as they conform to those practices which are seen to be essential to the survival of the society. Certainly the interpretation of the Supreme Court decision in 1972 with regard to Amish parochial schools would seem to support Bennett's contention. There is some disagreement about the degree to which cultural pluralism should be implemented and whether or not an individual or group should be allowed to choose freely to remain within the confines of their birthright community enclave (Gollnick and Chinn, 1986). In the meantime, legislation to protect individual and group rights, including those pertaining to ethnicity, is increasingly being passed to guarantee equality for all citizens (Tiedt and Tiedt, 1995).

The Government of Canada passed an Act of Multiculturalism in 1971, and surveys taken to determine public attitudes towards this action indicate a more favorable attitude since the time that the law was passed (Pawlowsky, 1992). Most provinces have enacted similar laws. This does not mean that prejudice and discrimination have been reduced by any means, but at least there are now laws in effect which can be appealed to when blatant instances of wrongful behavior involving race or ethnicity are enacted (Taylor, 1991). These findings would seem to indicate an enhanced acceptance of the principle of cultural pluralism in North America. All that remains now is for citizens to follow the lead of their governments and deliver equal treatment to all citizens.

A Model of Assimilation

Theories of ethnic change represent a variety of perspectives (Elliott & Fleras, 1992). Some theorists have predicted the demise and disappearance of ethnicity as a relevant force in societies undergoing urban-industrial changes, while others have emphasized social class and economic interests as the preferred basis for organization and differentiation in society (Fishman, 1989). Still others have perceived the persistence and growth of an urban and technologically-driven society (Isajiw, 1977). Classically, Gordon (1964) argued that a strong potential exists for ethnicities to disappear under assimilative pressures, while acknowledging the possibility for a modified and selective retention of ethnic identities. Although theorists have recently questioned the inevitable dissolution of traditional ethnocultural communities, the threat is still very real unless very deliberate, conscious and often significant adaptations are undertaken by a particular community. The popularized notion of discovering one's roots begun a decade or two ago has served to strengthen public interest in ethnicity but as a fad such campaigns tend to be temporary and fleeting, lacking any durable structural forms. Consequently, the Amish are faced with the challenge of deciding which of their values are worth preserving albeit perhaps in reinterpreted cultural forms more readily understood and perhaps appreciated by outsiders. At the outset this seems a very irrelevant exercise for any Amish to indulge in for it flies in the face of their most foundational belief. Life is not to be analyzed; it is to be lived in implicit obedience (Friesen, 1983).

In the near century since their arrival in North America nearly three centuries ago, the public image of the Amish has changed considerably. When they first arrived, they would have little to do with their fellow Americans, including their Mennonite cousins. Then, as the means of communication and travel improved, it became more difficult for them to live in seclusion. It was principally because of the difficulty in obtaining sufficient farmland for their young, that the Amish found it necessary to engage in other occupations as well. This brought them into more and more contact with the outside world. Contact per se, is not the only factor to consider; other relevant variables include: degrees of value differences between Amish and non-Amish, circumstances, intensity, frequency and hostility of contact; relative status of the agents of contact; who is dominant and who is submissive; and, whether the nature of the flow is reciprocal or non-reciprocal (Haviland, 1990).

There are many theories that have tried to describe the pluralistic nature of American society. The most prevailing theory espoused by sociologists, politicians and educators has been assimilation. Until recently, the trend in both the USA and Canada has been to attempt to assimilate all newcomers into the dominant society. It is the procedure by which microcultures become synonymous with the macroculture. Either cultural patterns that distinguished them from the macroculture have disappeared, or their distinctives have been adopted by the macroculture so that there is no longer a distinct and separate microculture. In some instances a combination of the two has occurred. According to Gordon (1964), the process of assimilation may involve seven stages until it is completed. While many North American ethnocultural communities have essentially completed all seven in their sojourn on the continent, the Amish have tried very hard to resist reaching even the first stage of the process. Still, there is evidence to suggest that they have significantly altered their lifestyle in some respects. They have not completely remained unaffected by either technological advances or social developments in the country. One might say that their assimilative experience has been to hover around the first two steps of Gordon's paradigm.

Gordon's model defines assimilation as the process of whereby dominant society imposes its culture, authority, values and institutions on the subordinate sector. Through assimilation the dominant group seeks to undermine the cultural basis of the subordinate sector, transform its membership allegiance to dominant forms, and thus facilitate their entry into mainstream society (Elliott & Fleras, 1992).

Indications that the processes identified in Gordon's model have been at play in the Amish community are substantial. This has simultaneously affected the way in which the community has been viewed by the public. Public perceptions of the negative kind seem to be related to the increased visibility of Amish presence, due to their population increase in some communities, and their relative economic success. Positive impressions of the Amish tend to emanate from tourist sectors and from the literature produced for tourists to read. These phenomena are supported by a general public feeling of nostalgia, of longing for a return to the "good ole days". Naturally, few people pursue this yearning; it is more fun just to romanticize it. The reality is that anyone wishing to adopt an Amish-like lifestyle in North America is certainly free to do so. It *can* be done.

Examples of Amish adjustment in several of the seven stages of Gordon's model supports the contention that, because of cultural shifts, and from the perspective of mainstream society, the Amish community in North America has begun the ascent (perhaps the Amish might view this process as a form of descent?) of reaching a relatively high degree of "ethnocultural respectability."

According to Gordon (1964), cultural assimilation will have been attained when the enthnocultural group in question has:

1. changed their cultural patterns (including religious belief and observance), to those of the host society. This is also called cultural or behavioral assimilation.
2. taken on large-scale primary group relationships with host society members, and entered fully into the societal network of groups and institutions, or societal structures. This may also be called structural assimilation.
3. intermarried and interbred fully with members of the host society. This may also be labelled marital assimilation.
4. developed a dominant, instead of a minority, sense of peoplehood or ethnicity. This may also be called identificational assimilation.
5. reached a point where they encounter no prejudice, which is called attitude reception assimilation.
6. reached a point where they encounter no discrimination, may also be labelled behavior reception assimilation.
7. do not raise by their demands concerning the nature of host societal (or civic) life any issues involving value and power conflict with the original members of their community. This is known as civic assimilation (70).

Applying the Model

A review of the literature on Amish, and relying on a personal degree of familiarity with the Amish community it is possible to identify some of the social and cultural changes that have occurred within the Amish community, particularly in the last few decades. At the outset it is useful to keep in mind that

> The Amish are not relics of a bygone era. They have maintained their identity by exhibiting great adaptability in a rapidly changing world. . . . Though not a model for all of society, the Amish demonstrate a different, yet successful way to be modern (Hostetler and Huntington, 1992, 120).

Gordon suggests that the first stage of cultural assimilation involves a change of cultural patterns, including religious beliefs and observances to those of host society. The Amish have only slightly changed their cultural habits, and certainly not their religion, to match that of dominant society. Although they are still basically an agrarian community, many of their young peoples are forced to take up employment in the non-Amish business world, working for other people or operating a private business. This has necessitated a certain amount of interaction with outsiders and no doubt provided

Amish youth with opportunities to learn about and perhaps adopt some "worldly" customs which they might otherwise never have known. Thus to engage in the "wild years" as an Amish youth today allows them to participate in quite different activities that those engaged in by their parents when they were of that age.

Studies in cultural maintenance classically identify the factors in cultural maintenance as geographic isolation, schooling, endogamy, institutional completeness, language, ideology and good opening and closing techniques (Friesen and Verigin, 1989). To varying degrees, isolationist societies throughout immigration history have tried to avail themselves of these "guarantees". Klimuska (1993) has identified ten factors that keep Amish society together, the first of which is schooling. By comparison, their cousins, the Hutterites, claim that one of *their* best guarantees for assuring cultural maintenance is their interpretation of the parochial school. Hutterite children learn the history and dictates of communal living in their mother tongue (German), diligently taught by a member of the community (Hostetler and Huntington, 1967). Other factors listed by Klimuska include: church discipline, avoidance of media, sense of community, family and kinship ties, reproduction through biological means only (not through evangelism), fundamental, uncompromising beliefs, a repugnance towards the institutions and practices of dominant society, and limited cultural integration. On most counts the Amish have managed very well to maintain a separate identity to the point of fulfilling the needs of their constituency without unduly interacting with the mainstream. On the positive side is education, particularly since the Amish have been awarded the right to organize and govern their own schools. The fundamental beliefs that govern Amish society also provide a firm unflinching foundation for the society, coupled with strict endogamy and evangelism solely through biological reproduction. On the taboo side of the ledger is a strongly-taught repugnance for "things of the world" bolstered by a fear of excommunication and shunning for those who get out of line.

To some extent structural assimilation of the Amish is evident from the fact that a component of Amish subsistence is achieved through the same means as other citizens. Many Amish are employed alongside their American or Canadian peers, they shop in the same stores, eat in the same restaurants, and do business in the same establishments as other citizens. Amish women sometimes have birthday parties, complete with cake, and the singing of "Happy Birthday" by restaurant staff, in local Pizza Huts. Amish have been known to vote (Yoder, 1993), to participate in civic protest meetings and to have had more than a single confrontation with government leaders (Thompson, 1993). Amish engage freely in worldly activities, and although they usually adopt the traditional lifestyle after baptism and marriage, they would indeed be atypical human beings if they remained forever unaffected after having tasted the "good life" of modern society in their "wilder" years. Besides, the Amish definition of "worldly" has evolved over time. The use of roller skates, once forbidden, now constitute a major means of transportation among many Lancaster Country youth. They appear to have been taken off the list of forbidden items like automobiles, cameras, tape recorders, television, films, showy houses, certain farm machinery, and attending high school (Kraybilll, 1990). Bicycles, by the way, though traditionally forbidden in many southeastern American Amish communities, are a mainstay in the small Amish settlement in northern Montana. Their use in Ohio is also on the upswing. Consistency, then, is not a major worry. No one is too concerned about the overall impression that outsiders may have of this inconsistency. They may wonder if all of these variations in behavior are to have their common origin in some obscure scripture passage. Still, human nature will out, and it is to be doubted that even very devout Amish would deny that some of the pleasures of the world were indeed enjoyable when they once indulged in them.

Conclusion

Perhaps one of the reasons why the apparent cultural gap between the dominant society and the Amish lifestyle remains so wide is that both societies are developing at about the same rate. While technological and social advances are the forte of modern society, changes of this type also occur in the Amish community. To properly appreciate the magnitude of the gap that *might* exist between the "classic" Old Order Amish lifestyle and dominant society one might consider studying the lifestyles of some of the conservative breakaway groups which leave the Old Order to return to more traditional ways, that is, Swartzentruber Amish, and those in Buchanan County, Iowa and the "Nebraska" group in Mifflin County Pennsylvania (Nolt, 1992). Like other Anabaptist groups, the Amish faithfully follow their interpretation of the biblical injunction that "every believer is her or her own priest" and continue to carry on the splintering tradition (Gingerich, 1972). Causes of splits are not necessarily deeply grounded in theological debate; they may be based on such a tangible items as a wedding ring, a pair of spectacles, a necktie, rubber suspenders, leather belts, barber haircuts or a woman's hair style (Schreiber, 1990).

Our secular orientation may not have within its scope the ability to fully appreciate the extent to which the Old Order Amish project an aura of the sacred to every aspect of their lives. Modern North American citizens are basically involved in the throes of a long-standing campaign to eliminate anything that even smacks of the sacred in our deliberations about human society, the world and the universe. It may not hurt to study at least one alternative explanation of these workings, and the Amish provide a ready model.

Although perhaps a bit overzealous in admiration, one Kent student offered this final tribute to the Amish:

> I am very envious of the Amish because I feel today, society in general, would be at a greater advantage if we would implement even a small percentage of the customs of the Amish. The Amish are very helpful to each other; they look out for each other, and their main focus is helping and caring about one another.

In the interests of building a better world through respect for the individual *and* the community, and satisfy the persistent human quest for alternatives, it is entirely conceivable that everyone can benefit from a further study of Amish philosophy. Such a search may even result in discovering the implication of the Amish expression, reiterated here by William A. Yoder,

We are not Amish, we are Christians. Amish is just a nickname. We don't need to be ashamed that people call us that but we shouldn't build on the name Amish (Hostetler, 1992, 265).

References

Bennett, Christine L. (1995). *Comprehensive Multicultural Education: Theory and Practice.* third edition. Boston: Allyn and Bacon.

Driedger, Leo. ed. (1989). *The Ethnic Factor: Identity in Diversity.* Toronto, ON: McGraw-Hill.

Durkheim, Emile. (1976). *The Elementary Forms of the Religious Life.* London: George, Allen and Unwin.

Elliott, Jean Leonard and Augie Fleras. (1992). *Unequal Relations: An Introduction to Race and Ethnic Dynamics in Canada.* Scarborough, ON: Prentice-Hall.

Fishman, Joshua. (1989). *Language and Ethnicity in Minority Sociolinguistic Matters.* Clevedon, England: Multilingual Matters.

Friesen, John W. (1983). *Schools With a Purpose.* Calgary, AB: Detselig Enterprises.

Friesen, John W. (1993). *When Cultures Clash: Case Studies in Multiculturalism.* second edition. Calgary, AB: Temeron Books.

Friesen, John W. (1995). *Pick One: A User-Friendly Guide to Religion.* Calgary, AB: Temeron Books.

Friesen, John W. and Michael M. Verigin. (1989). *The Community Doukhobors: A People in Transition.* Ottawa, ON: Borealis.

Gingerich, Orland. (1972). *The Amish of Canada.* Waterloo, ON: Conrad Press.

Gollnick, Donna M., and Philip C. Chinn. (1986). *Multicultural Education in a Pluralistic Society.* Columbus, OH: Charles E. Merrill Publishing Company.

Gordon, Milton. (1964). *Assimilation in American life.* New York: Oxford University Press.

Haviland, William A. (1990). *Cultural Anthropology.* sixth edition. Fort Worth, TX: Holt, Rinehart and Winston, Inc.

Henslin, James M. (1995). *Sociology: A Down-to-Earth Approach.* Boston: Allyn and Bacon.

Hostetler, John A. (1993). *Amish Society,* fourth edition. Baltimore, MD: The Johns Hopkins University Press.

Hostetler, John A. (1992). *Amish Roots: A Treasury of History, Wisdom, and Lore.* Baltimore, MD: The Johns Hopkins University Press.

Hostetler, John A. and Gertrude Enders Huntington. (1967). *The Hutterites of North America.* New York: Holt, Rinehart and Winston.

Hostetler, John A. and Gertrude Enders Huntington. (1992). *Amish Children: Education in the Family, School, and Community.* second edition. Fort Worth, TX: Harcourt Brace Jovanovich College Publishers.

Isajiw, Wsevolod W. (1977). Olga in Wonderland: Ethnicity in Technological Society. *Canadian ethnic studies,* IX:1, 77–85.

Klimuska, Ed. (1993). 10 Key Factors that "Glue" the Amish Society. *Lancaster New Era,* July 21, 1993, A12, A6.

Kraybill, Donald B. (1990). *The Riddle of Amish Culture.* Baltimore, MD: The Johns Hopkins University Press.

Marx, Karl and Friedrich Engels. (1967). *The Communist Manifesto.* New York: Pantheon. First published in 1848.

Nolt, Stephen. (1992). *A History of the Amish.* Intercourse, PA: Good Books.

Pawlowsky, Alexandra, ed. (Autumn, 1992). 1991 Attitude Survey Multiculturalism and Citizenship: Highlights of Major Findings. *CESA Bulletin,* XIX:2,1–5.

Schreiber, William I. (1990). *Our Amish Neighbors.* Wooster, OH: The College of Wooster Press.

Sorokin, Pitirim. (1947). *Society, Culture and Personality.* New York: Harper & Brothers.

Spencer, Metta. (1990). *Foundations of Modern Sociology.* Scarborough, ON: Prentice Hall, Canada, Inc.

Taylor, K.W. (1991). Racism in Canadian Immigration Policy. *Canadian ethnic studies,* XXIII:1, 1–20.

Tiedt, Pamela L. and Iris M. Tiedt. (1995). *Multicultural Teaching: A Handbook of Activities, Information, and Resources.* fourth edition. Boston: Allyn and Bacon.

Thompson, Dennis L. (1993). Canadian Government Relations. *The Amish and the State.* Donald B. Kraybill, ed. Baltimore, MD: The Johns Hopkins University Press, 235–250.

Tönnies, Ferdinand. (1988), *Community and Society (Gemeinschaft und Gesellschaft).* New Brunswick, NJ: Transaction. First published in 1887.

Toynbee, Arnold. (1946). *A Study of History.* New York: Oxford University

Yoder, Paton. (1993). The Amish View of the State. *The Amish and the State.* Donald B. Kraybill, ed. Baltimore, MD: The Johns Hopkins University Press, 23–42.

Chapter 5

Perceptions of Amish Society: Youth and Education

Radcliffe-Brown (1957) once observed that every culture or society has a kind of functional unity in which all the parts work together without producing too many conflicts that cannot be resolved or regulated. Durkheim (1933) saw societies as composed of many parts, each with its own function. When all the parts operate effectively, society may be conceived of as "normal". If they do not function in keeping with their designated purpose, society may be said to be dysfunctional or in a state of pathology. Merton (1968) and others rejected this view on grounds that it is too simplistic, and these sociologists have contended that some cultural elements may actually be dysfunctional to a society's operation. Merton suggested that some parts of society may actually be dysfunctional, having consequences that undermine the system's equilibrium. This view historically contributed towards a new vocabulary for the social sciences, including such terms as *social function*, which refers to the observable consequences of a repeated social event, and *dysfunction*, which implies that consequences may be negative when the level of satisfaction of individual needs or group requirements is reduced. This may tend to lessen the adaptation or adjustment of the system.

To those not familiar with the rationale for the workings of a particular cultural configuration, may deem some of its practices to be dysfunctional; to outsiders some cultural processes may even appear to be working against the basic objectives of the system. Two additional terms are helpful here, namely *manifest functions* and *latent functions*. The former are *intended functions*; they are recognized by participants in the system and are seen to contribute to the adjustment or adaptation of the system. *Latent functions*, on the other hand are those that are neither intended nor recognized. The same may be said for latent dysfunctions in that they may do unwanted harm to the system (Henslin, 1993). These terms are merely part of Merton's conceptual apparatus for functional analysis. It may be helpful to outline the basic steps of Merton's paradigm for studying social systems.

1. Identify precisely those items within the area under study which have observable consequences for surrounding units;

2. Specify the purposes and intentions of the actors involved;
3. Distinguish between manifest and latent functions, and between functions and dysfunctions;
4. Note which units are affected by the objective consequences of the items being investigated;
5. If possible, identify the needs of individuals concerned and the functional requirements of groups;
6. Specify the mechanisms by which functions are mediated.
7. Examine possible functional alternatives and the limitations imposed by the structural context;
8. Investigate sources of structural change, especially in relation to dysfunctions; and,
9. Validate the analysis, if possible, by means of systematic comparison with similar social situations (Mulkay, 1971, 103–104).

There are, of course sociologists who perceive of societies in other than structural/functionalist terms, one of which may be labelled the conflict perspective. Karl Marx is often credited with originating this view, based on the following assumptions: societal change is inevitable, it is a result of conflict among the various parts of the system, economic structures are important in determining societal structures, and the inter-relations among the various parts must be taken into account in identifying or delineating the impact of change (Marx, 1906; Hagedorn, 1994). Marx's paradigm is useful in helping to understand the interplay of conflict and power between the older and younger generations in Amish society. It is relatively easy to identify forms of change in Amish society and, as in other societies, conflict and dissension is always present as well. Moreover, change in Amish society, no matter how slowly it is introduced, may be attributable to specific elements or factors some of them directly related to the manipulation of power.

The Old Order Amish community provides a classic yet accessible arena in which to elaborate in practical terms how certain cultural practices may serve the purpose of being either functional or serving as impediments to achieving their society's goals. It may be presumptuous to suggest that such activities can be identified, let alone understood, and it is helpful to remember that in the study of cultural patterns other that one's own, understanding is the first priority. In the case of the Amish, it is might be safe to say that it is doubtful that even their own members always fully understand their various ways; after all, their obligation is to obey the dictates of the *Ordnung.* The rules of the *Ordnung* comprise a body of unwritten truth put together under the direction of a group of church leaders who originate them through consensus. All members of the local *Gemeindung* (church body) must know and obey the rules.

Rules as Social Control

Robert Redfield (1941) suggested that folk societies are small, closely-integrated social units or by-aggregates which have already worked out satisfactory mutual adjustments. New items do not appear with great frequency, and when they do the society has plenty of time to test them and assimilate them into its pre-existing pattern. In such cultures the core constitutes almost the whole. In this context, Hostetler (1993) notes that the Amish are in some ways analogous to a miniature commonwealth, for their members claim to be ruled by the same law of love and redemption. Still, they are a church, a community, a spiritual union, and at the same time a conservative religion whose members practice simple and austere living. They are also a familial, entrepreneurial system, and an adaptive community.

In seeking to maintain what is essentially a 18th century pattern of living, the Old Order Amish regulate all community and individual decisions. These are to be obeyed without question, and when an infraction occurs, members of the *Ordnung* will meet to discuss individual cases of indiscretion. Rules may vary from one constituency to another but seeming paradoxes and blatant contradictions are of concern only to outsiders. Infractions of the rules may include such diverse behaviors as unduly brightening up a horse harness, attending a meeting of another group of Mennonites or other branch of Amish, or employing forbidden technology such as rubber tires on horse-drawn farm equipment. Sometimes changes to the rules are made in order to accommodate unusual circumstances, as in the case of an Amish community at Clarita, Oklahoma, where Amish leaders recently voted to allow tractors for fieldwork because of the hard soil in the area. The decision to use tractors led some traditionalists to leave the community because they interpreted the action as dangerous because such relaxing of rules might tempt members to break away from the mainstream of Amish society. The new use of tractors could mean increased mobility, commercialized farming and increased debt. Thus the more orthodox faction felt they had no choice but to break away themselves *(Mennonite Reporter*, 1995).

Amish rule-breakers are usually admonished for their misconduct, and often find themselves brought up before the church body without advance warning. Hostetler (1993) tells the story of one Amish individual in Pennsylvania who was excommunicated for various intimated offenses. When he tried to reconcile with the church he was refused on grounds that he "talked back" to his accusers and to the ordained Amish officials at his "trial". He allegedly committed some offence in connection with his progressive farming practices, but these were never clearly explicated at his hearing. When he moved his family to another state and joined another Amish fellowship, his bishop back home found out about it and wrote to the local bishop admonishing him to excommunicate the man and his family. The bishop promptly did so—no questions asked. The farmer then made four unsuccessful trips back to Pennsylvania to attempt a reconciliation with his home church. Still, to no avail. The bottom line was that anyone wishing to be reinstated after excommunication should never "talk back" to his superiors. "No amount of argument, justification, or logic will aid in reconciliation. A submissive attitude is absolutely necessary" (Hostetler, 1993, 347).

A cohesive social unit such as Amish society appears to foster a high degree of effective social control; it governs one's work, religious convictions, family life, and other aspects of living. What manages to be projected is the impression of a very smoothly functioning entity. Even so, however, conservative analysts estimate that about 20 percent of Amish young people choose to leave that way of life and associate with others; usually the new association is with a Mennonite-related community following a similar pattern of life. Kraybill (1990a) suggests that the current rate of leaving is higher than 12 percent but notes that Amish leaders believe that the rate has declined over the last two decades. In an earlier edition of his work, Hostetler (1980) found the rate of attrition to be as high as 18–24 percent in Lancaster County, and a study in Illinois found that the number of young people who rejected the Old Order way of life was as high as 51 percent (Nagata, 1968).

Though the image that the Amish attempt to portray is that they do not allow or encourage the abandonment of their faith by their young, the fact is that many do leave the Amish community. Basically this is due to the built-in generational gap that the culture fosters between youth and their parents. The following discussion may shed some light on the factors which might be responsible for this phenomenon.

The Anabaptist Vision

Reasons for the relatively high attrition rate among Amish young people may partially be grounded in Anabaptist history. As is the case with all religious groups claiming an historical connection to the work of such leaders as Menno Simons, Conrad Grebel, Felix Manz, Georg Blaurock, Jacob Ammann, and others, the notion that "the individual is his own priest" is adhered to by the Amish (Smith, 1957). This principle accounts for the lack of a central authority for the "denomination" and the maintenance of local autonomy for the church. It may also help explain why parents fail to squash what are termed "rowdy" activities among their youth. Their teaching on nonresistance prevents them from taking coercive measures even against their own children. Only when they deem the offence of their offspring to be "severe" will they report their activities to law enforcement officials. Amish, after all, like other Anabaptists, are pacifists. The irony is that many of the activities of the early Anabaptist leaders were anything but passive or gentle. Jacob Amman, for example, was a very strict leader in banning certain forms of apparel and insisting on simple grooming. In one instance, though he had no official authority to do so, he excommunicated a whole group of ministers. He even had a name for outside sympathizers who favored his people, calling them intruders who were "trying to enter the sheep fold some other way. . . . there is but one people who are the bride of Christ" (Hostetler, 1993, 344).

The aggressive form of pacifism practiced by Ammann seems to have deep historical roots. Around 1525, after his conversion from Catholicism, Georg Blaurock blocked the local priest from entering the church pulpit on grounds that he was not preaching the Gospel. When the pastor began preaching anyway, Blaurock kept interrupting him. Then he banged a stick on a bench and yelled, "my house shall be called a house of prayer, but you have made it a den of thieves". Finally, a church official threatened to call the police. Blaurock and his Anabaptist colleagues were often involved in boisterous debates with the Catholic counterparts (Ruth, 1975, 108). Their stated beliefs may have included humility, peace-making and pacifism, but they probably would have claimed that the times in which they lived demanded forceful preaching coupled with bold, direct confrontation. No doubt they would have found it hard to convince their public that they were "the quiet in the land".

The Anabaptist concept of the individual as his or her own priest compares easily with the American-prized notion of individualism. The difference between the two conceptualizations is with regard to child-rearing. In many Anabaptist homes, including Amish, the child in the teen years is awarded a measure of freedom from church dictates. Then, when the "age of accountability" is attained, the individual becomes responsible for his or her own actions. No one comments much on this somewhat mystical phenomenon, because, apparently no one really knows when the "age of accountability" is reached. It varies with the individual and no Anabaptist theologian would probably be willing to conjecture as to what exactly that age might be. The general understanding is that when an individual reaches this stage in life, he or she makes their vows before the church and is baptized. Among the Amish (and Hutterites) this often happens just before marriage. Other Mennonite groups are more flexible in their interpretations of the age of accountability and have sometimes recognized it as occurring even in the pre-teen years. Since baptism is a requirement for marriage, the reality of Amish practice is that many young people probably put off baptism as long as they can because they enjoy their "worldly" lifestyle so much (Nolt, 1992).

The Generation Gap

The tenacity of Anabaptist beliefs and the severe measures of excommunication and shunning have served through the centuries as effective means for maintaining adherence to the group. The dysfunctional element has been the gap that has built up between parents and youth during the years that the latter have been allowed to "run around". Although the Amish family offers a closely-knit set of activities including doing chores, making clothing and canning, worshipping together, planting and harvesting crops, from a purely sociological vantage point, there appears to exist a significant gap between parents and youth. This is particularly evident on two fronts, in courtship practices and in the socialization component endorsed by the church. Since the social activities that Amish people may participate in are quite limited—church activities, visiting, attending auction sales or purchasing supplies—the only additional event which is amenable to courtship is the Sunday night song fest in some neighbor's barn. Traditionally this event featured hymn-sings but several sources indicate that the current selection of music is similar to that offered on any radio station—western, popular, or even rock-and-roll. In fact, a hard-bound songbook published by the Gordonville [Amish] Print Shop contains a variety of sacred-secular song titles (all without copyright permission): "Will the Circle be Unbroken, Jack the Cowboy, Are You Washed in the Blood, Yellow Rose of Texas, He's Got the Whole World in His Hands", and so on, including several German selections (*Schwartzs' Song Book*, 1980).

Some Sunday night hoedowns have featured Amish youth playing forbidden musical instruments, and even outside groups have occasionally been hired to perform rock music. Accompanying activities frequently include drinking, smoking and "carrying on". At times when parents feel matters are out of control they will call the local police and ask them to shut down a particularly wild Sunday night part—which may even feature liquor, rock music and even the occasional fist-fight. As one Amish parent described it, "We have to tolerate immature behavior with the expectation that they'll eventually grow up, and become mature and responsible. It's nothing more than normal adolescent behavior" (Kirkpatrick, 1981, B16). Modern, child-oriented, urban middle class parents might be driven to call a "talk-in" with their offspring about unapproved behavior, but not the Amish. In the final analysis, the youth have done nothing really wrong as long as they have not yet taken their church vows. This condoning spirit is applied to other areas as well. Amish youth occasionally resort to vandalism to "let off steam." On occasion, the local police turn a blind eye if the offenses are small (Nagata, 1968). The annual "Florida reunion" described by Hostetler (1993) demonstrates another non-parent approved form of Amish "revelry". It includes the renting of a camp or resort center (compete with security guards) for use by hundreds of Amish youth to party with beer and "wild" music. Only trusted members are admitted and the whole event is apparently executed without parental knowledge. Many male Amish youth own cars, some of which are stored at the homes of more liberal neighbors, but a few may even be accommodated in their parents' yard. While drinking and smoking are generally frowned on in Amish communities these practices are overlooked on the part of unbaptized youth simply because they have not yet committed themselves to abstention. When travelling in Amish country, if one looks hard, one can discover groups of young Amish men indulging in various "forbidden activities" such as car driving, drinking and smoking. "A lot of Amish have cars," a youthful driver says matter-of-factly, "My parents don't like it. But they got over it. They can't keep bugging you. They don't want to send you away from home. They know we'll get wild and won't come back" (Kirkpatrick, 1981, B16). The community explanation for this behavior may be that the youth are simply "sowing their wild oats" before settling down. They may also be from a Beachy community who do allow cars, although they may have more severe restrictions against indulging in the use of liquor or tobacco. At least one of the more western conferences of the Amish have pointed out the apparent contradiction of Amish displeasures with smoking when many of their Lancaster farms grow tobacco (Hostetler, 1993).

One of the reasons why Amish adolescent rowdiness occurs is that Amish youth are psychologically abandoned by their parents at a time when they need them most (Hostetler, 1993). To outsiders it appears as though these youth are heavily indoctrinated, but the truth is that they are often lacking in role models when confronted with moral imponderables. Thus, Amish youth, at least partially abandoned by their parents at a time when communication process should flow smoothly between parent and child. Essentially, they are released into the "world" to taste and test its pleasures with the expectation that they will reject them and elect to accept the Amish value system.

Amish society justifies its maintenance of this generation gap. The historical Anabaptist position, which was intended to safeguard the concept of personal choice in identifying with the Christian faith, has in effect reversed its earlier function and induced dysfunctional reverberations. When and if the young people eventually elect to join the church, they are expected to abandon their worldly way of life and take up the traditional ways of the Amish including farming. In many cases this virtually *does* "happen over night". In the meantime, however, many will not pledge allegiance to the church, no doubt because they have been influenced by the "non-religious" way of life that they have been able to pursue with such wild abandon.

The belief that one must make a personal decision about his faith after reaching the age of accountability at times seems to work dysfunctionally for the Amish. Their youth are not subject to church sanctions until they say their vows. Parents, not wishing to interfere unduly in the decision-making deliberations of their children, allow a great deal of latitude in their behavior. Communication between parents and youth is minimal and youth often do things behind their parents' back. Many observers believe that this is one of the primary reasons why so many Amish youth leave way their way of life. The youth are simply allowed too much freedom before they are required to join the church and become subject to its sanctions. Thus they too strongly buy into the "worldly" lifestyle and remain with it. Kraybill (1990b) contends that Amish youth only *perceive* their choice to leave the community. Since they are raised as Amish, they rarely actually leave the community. Their choice to leave is therefore a *perceived* choice, not an *real* choice.

Mainline religious traditions, like the Methodists, Roman Catholics, Episcopalians or Presbyterians do not generally experience this form of religiously-inspired generation gap. Their interpretation of infant baptism and confirmation preclude this. In these denominations the focus is on the spiritual development of children within the church context from the moment of their initial christening or baptism. They are then to be raised within the general Christian environment of the church family with equal responsibility to live out the ideals of the faith. Confirmation merely affords individuals the opportunity to confirm their already established place in Christendom. Naturally, this position is adamantly rejected by contemporary Anabaptists who still visualize infant baptism as connected with the concept of a state church, something their ancestors in the faith originally fought against. Thus the dilemma of the generation gap may continue indefinitely among the Anabaptist groups, particularly the Amish.

The apparent generation gap between Amish adults and youth probably concerns no one as much as outsiders whose orientation is heavily framed by modern child-rearing practices. Anthropologically speaking, the phenomenon of the Amish generation-gap might be labelled a cultural discontinuity of classic description. For most of their youthful years individuals are allowed to indulge in a heavy diet of worldliness, by Amish standards; then they take instruction, say their vows, and become orthodox believers. It would be inaccurate to say that Amish parents are not concerned about the worldly habits of their young people, but because their orientation to proceed in such matters, as well as in any other, is an acceptance of tradition, and there is little chance that the apparent gap will be eliminated. To the Amish the gap probably does not even exist. It is the way things are, and things are not to be questioned.

In contrast to the social dissent that dominates the parent-youth relations in Amish society, is the manner in which hardship and death are dealt with by the community. The barn-raisings of the Amish are well known in regions where they live; when a the barn on a family farm burns down the neighbors descend upon the site and reconstruct it, sometimes within a day or two. Since the Amish do not generally believe in buying insurance policies they have replaced the need for them with traditional friendliness and helpfulness. Similarly, when death comes to the Amish, the community handles it as they have for over 300 years (Bryer, 1979). In this context, the community ministers to individuals at their point of need and they are never abandoned.

Amish Schooling

Modern civilization likes to pride itself with its achievements in education, positing the image that schooling is effectively tuned to socializing students in a way that will prepare them for the roles they will fill on reaching adulthood. Too often, however, educators have to deal with the byproducts of such institutional training as peer group conflicts, delinquency, school dropouts, problem children and inadequate school-community relations. Many times it is through no fault of the school that these situations emerge, but much of the blame will still be placed on that institution and on its teachers. Because schooling has to contend with and try to be relevant to diverse kinds of groups and social philosophies in a given society, it becomes impossible to completely appease more than a few of them. Thus to suggest that the school is integrated with society would be inaccurate. At best the school can serve only a segment of society and, some would say, inefficiently at that.

Smaller components of any social organization are frequently better integrated than society as such, particularly when the flavor and constitution of that component is fairly uniform throughout. When Amish society is utilized as an example of such a social component, it will be seen to comprise a well-integrated social unit particularly as far as the school is concerned. There may be dysfunctional elements in the system, for example, the seeming generation gap referred to earlier, but schooling is not one of them. In fact, in Amish society, the school may be viewed as a synthesizing factor, consistently and harmoniously promoting the goals of their way of life.

Perhaps the most successful experiences of the Amish with regard to effective cultural maintenance is with regard to schooling (Friesen, 1983). Although the particular arrangement with which they operate is only a few decades old, the Amish now sponsor a series of private, non-state-funded schools in every state they occupy. On a broader scale, the issue of educating children of ethnic minorities has proven to be a most perplexing one in North American history, and the policy that everyone should go to the same school in order to learn to be a well-adjusted citizen has not always operated without complexities. A few specific cases may serve to demonstrate the problems of an educational policy bent on assimilating minorities. The most obvious one is that of North American First Nations people whose offspring were targeted by would-be civilizers (religious and secular) virtually from the time that the first Europeans set foot on the North American continent. Finally, as the last decade has witnessed, Native leaders have risen up to decry the incessant destruction of their civilization and morale and have insisted on participating in the planning of Native education. Blatant attempts at assimilation, while not completely put to rest, have been at least partially restrained through the establishment of Native-operated schools, accompanied by the implementation of a modified and more relevant curriculum, locally-determined policy, and the preparation of Native teachers. In the mid-sixties the Navajo tribe in Arizona founded the Rough Rock School which featured the first North American Indian-originated, designed and operated local school. Since then replicas of this school have sprung up on Indian reservations all across Canada and the USA.

Other ethnocultural groups have experienced similar insensitivity in their children's education, particularly the Chinese, Japanese, and Doukhobors in British Colombia, and the Hutterites in the prairie states and provinces (Friesen, 1993). The Hutterites have managed to procure a unique kind of educational arrangement on their colonies. They run their own private schools, utilize a state-approved curriculum and still pay public school taxes on top of that. Still other ethnic minorities have sought to perpetuate aspects of their cultural heritage and language through the establishment of special part-time schools that are dedicated to that purpose.

Historical Developments

Amish education received its most severe onslaught, at least in terms of publicity, in the State of Iowa in 1965. At that time state officials at Oelwein, Iowa, decided one day to force 40 Amish youngsters to enroll at the public school. Anxious to close down the illegal private school established by the local community, officials decided that the law of compulsory public education had to be enforced, so on November 19, 1965, a special school bus loaded with authorities arrived at the Amish schoolhouse where 17 carloads of reporters from all over the nation awaited them. The event ended with the officers chasing pupils into the nearby corn fields trying to catch them and put them on the bus. Two children were caught. That day the national newspapers carried pictures of the scene with appropriate captions featuring the word "freedom" in bold letters. After this embarrassing incident, state officials set about preparing the way for legalization of Amish private schools (Erickson, 1975).

On May 15, 1972, the United States Supreme Court ruled in favor of the Amish. The decision ended a series of arrests and jailings of Amish in various parts of the United States. One Amish individual, LeRoy Garber, was harassed out of the state of Kansas for not enrolling his daughter in a public high school, and another Amish person, Adin Yutzy, paid a large fine, sold his farm, and moved to another state in order to escape "school trouble." Only in Kentucky did the court find an Amish "not guilty" of violating the school attendance law because he had acted "on the basis of religious conscience" (Hostetler and Huntington, 1971, 98–99).

A related factor that demonstrates the way that public education has infringed on the Amish way of life is that in many cases Amish young people, thrust into the value system of public schools, find themselves to be no match for the reasoning of the non-Amish peers and thus give in to the appeal of the school culture. Following this experience a large number of Amish youth migrate to the new-found world of freedom and pleasure. Thus, public education has proven to be more than a threat to Amish values; it is dysfunctional in the fullest sense of the word.

Amish Parochial Schools

In Pennsylvania there are around 250 one-room schoolhouses operated by the Amish, usually under the direction of a young Amish woman having only eight years of formal schooling. Ohio has about 150 such schools. In a few cases men may be assigned to teach, and there is at least one school in which a non-Amish person functions as teacher. In one instance a non-Amish teacher was hired who possessed a Master's Degree, but insofar as the Amish were concerned, the quality of the instruction she offered would not exceed that of the instruction offered by regular Amish teachers. Suitability for teaching in Amish society is best understood by contrasting the role expectations of an Amish teacher with that of the typical North American suburban school teacher. In the Amish situation the teacher is much involved with parents, children and the general community. She is one of them; the moral expectations of her behavior are very high. Unstated and nonverbal conveyors of information are extremely important. By contrast, in a secondary society, what the teacher does on his or her own time is no one's business (Hostetler and Huntington, 1992).

The State of Pennsylvania has approved Amish-run schools from grades one to eight and pretty well all Amish children are enrolled in them. The Amish petitioned for such an arrangement when, distraught by the implication of progressive education of the nineteen thirties, they realized that the consolidation of the schools constituted a threat to their way of life and they decided that appropriate action needed to be taken. Not all of the Amish were able to see this immediately, but over the years nearly all of them eventually rallied behind their leaders in support of the movement. The decision of the American Governmental Department of Education to abolish prayer and the mention of the Deity in the classroom undoubtedly helped in making the final decision.

Even after the Amish were granted the privilege of operating their own elementary schools, they still had to contend with the high school factor. The Amish see no need for education beyond minimal literacy. Even if someone does leave the faith, they argue that the skills and work ethic learned as Amish are so valuable that these individuals would never be a burden on society (Beachy, 1992). The state requirement for schooling past grade eight was accommodated for the Amish by the government in allowing students who had finished elementary schooling to work on their parents' farms as a kind of vocational educational period, with the students giving an account of themselves and the activities in which they took part. The program was established in October of 1955 but the requirements have been relaxed since. In its earlier stages an Amish teacher held classes for three hours per week for a dozen or so students of high school age. The youth submitted diaries of their work activities around the farm but also studied a bit of math, English, and spelling. Attendance records were then submitted to the state (Kraybill, 1990a). Gideon Fisher (1978), a Lancaster County Amish farmer and writer, describes the governmental-sanctioned Amish high school alternative this way:

> . . . the state offered a vocational plan which was accepted by the Amish brethren. After a child was through the eighth grade and was fourteen years of age, he or she was then consigned to make out a written report (in diary form) of the kind of work they did each day of the week, for the boys was

probably farming, milking cows, mowing grass, baling hay, etc., for the girls were doing housework, cooking, baking, canning, sewing, etc. This report was then forwarded to the teacher who kept classes five hours each week, which included teaching of mathematics. This system satisfied the state, the law was not violated, and is considered educational. The children are released from this class at the age of fifteen (315).

A similar program was developed in Ohio and still prevails. As a "high school" requirement, boys often carry on some type of project that makes money for them. Some raise hogs, rabbits, poultry, dairy cattle or even homing pigeons. Others raise special breeds of dogs such as Beagles, Rottweilers and Elkhounds. Female students engage in home economics-type projects such as sewing, crocheting and knitting, babysitting, first-aid and CPR, table setting and manners, and meal planning (Mykrantz, 1994).

Amish Teachers

Teachers of Amish schools are viewed as extension workers of the home and church. These people are selected with great care, and their qualifications are personal rather than academic. In keeping with the oral tradition of the Amish a teacher (usually female) teaches with her whole life. She must be respected by the community and function in keeping with the goals of the community. Her confessed faith and practice must be approved by the *Ordnung* and be demonstrative of the character traits which Amish esteem: humility, obedience, steadfastness and love for others (Hostetler and Huntington, 1971). Discipline is left to the discretion of the teacher because Amish philosophy is that if the child receives punishment in school, he will be a candidate for an additional dose on his arrival home. This understanding between parents and children has a very positive effect on school behavior. Parents usually visit the school once or twice during the school year, coming without prior knowledge of the teacher or the children. In some schools the teacher may ask parents to attend, a different family each week. This is to help the children develop the feeling that their parents are concerned enough about school to visit frequently (Fisher and Stahl, 1986).

Amish school curriculum heavily favors factual knowledge in both subject matter and student performance, even though the foregoing virtues are perceived as primary. Teacher content and methodology are outlined in the regularly published Guidelines furnished by the Old Order (*Guidelines In Regards to the Old Order Amish or Mennonite Parochial Schools 1978–1980*). This brief booklet outlines Amish aims for education, the Amish educational creed, and recommendations for teaching subject matter. Each school district is run by a board of Amish men composed of three members; it is they who select the teacher. Once approved by the board, the teacher must serve a three-year probationary period and meet regularly for instruction with other Amish teachers who have taught effectively for at least twenty years. At the end of the three-year period, successfully teachers are granted an "Amish Diploma" produced by the local print shop.

Amish people pay school taxes in the same manner as other Pennsylvanians and operate their own schools from additional monies raised for that purpose. Teachers are paid by the board and salaries are low. Class size in the schools is around the thirty pupil mark. If the teacher has to be absent for a day, pay is deducted. There are no fringe benefits, no additional privileges and no job security. It seems ironic that a society that allegedly reveres the proper instruction of their young as much as the Amish purport to, places so little monetary value on the duty of teaching. The average income of the Amish farmer in Lancaster County greatly exceeds that of the Amish teacher, and still there are usually enough teachers to go around. Like the majority of North Americans, the Amish see teaching as low-cost service profession, requiring dedication mainly on the part of the teacher.

Amish Curriculum

The curriculum of the Amish one-room school is taken directly from old school texts published in the nineteen thirties and forties. The Print Shop at Gordonville, under the direction of the various school boards, has obtained permission to reprint and bind old curricula used in the former American "little red schoolhouse". For example, one arithmetic class uses the 1934 Strayer-Upton *Practical Arithmetics* textbook. On the list of desired curricula, math ranks number one. Here is the list of approved subjects:

- Mathematics-Arithmetic
- Geography and History
- Health and Safety rules
- German writing, reading and spelling as per home community instructions
- Phonics
- Vocal Music
- Penmanship
  (*Guidelines In Regards to the Old Order Amish or Mennonite Parochial Schools 1978–1980*).

Noticeably missing from the above list are science and social studies, both considered by the Amish as an anathema to Christian faith. Science they regard as in opposition to the creation account and hence, highly suspect; social studies they consider unnecessary because too much about the world will be learned by the pupil and thus he or she may be drawn away from the Old Order way of life.

Some of the recommended rules for children in the *Guidelines* are quite predictable and strict:

- Teasing of children not allowed
- No nicknames
- No by-words allowed
- No competitive games with other people
- When bell rings, all playing stops immediately, and children go to their desks
- All pupils shall be modestly dressed. [sic]
  (*Guidelines In Regards to the Old Order Amish or Mennonite Parochial Schools 1978–1980*).

Lest the impression be gained that only students are targeted for instruction, Hostetler and Huntington (1992) paraphrase a list of suggestions for new teachers entitled "Pitfalls to Avoid":

- Don't be bashful. . . .
- Don't be bossy. . . .
- Don't be openly suspicious. . . .
- Don't be afraid to admit a mistake. . . .
- Don't be afraid to say, "I don't know". . . .
- Don't be too chummy with your pupils. . . .
- Never belittle a pupil in the presence of his peers. . . .
- Don't expect to become a teacher overnight . . . (80).

Young teachers are cautioned that the voice of authority is not loud, overbearing or sarcastic. It is firm and loving and commands respect. Sometimes words are not even necessary; a stern look may suffice. Rules for children when school is in session include the forbidding of whispering, gum-chewing, loud talking, throwing of paper, unruliness or exchanging of desks without permission from the teacher. The teacher's word is the final authority and she is to be obeyed without question. After all, she is the parents' and community's representative during school hours, and the school is an extension of Amish life.

Amish School Life

The student population of Amish schools in some communities may include pupils from conservative Old Order Mennonite children as well as Amish, and on this important matter the two groups work together in harmony. Rarely do members of these groups intermarry, and if this should happen the couple would have to choose an allegiance to *either* the Old Order or the conservative Mennonite Church. The Amish person who marries a Mennonite, after having made vows in an Amish congregation, is excommunicated and shunned. As pupils grow older they must be very careful to maintain strict social lines.

Observing an Amish classroom in action is a delightful experience. Pupils work diligently, but are cheerful. The teacher functions so as to leave no doubt as to who is in charge, although her manner is kind and caring. A regular feature of classroom life is drill, a time when the pupils of all eight grades march to the front of the classroom in groups and engage in a spelling bee or answer questions in geography or history, either individually or on a free-for-all basis, put to them by the teacher. Pupils giving the right answer are allowed to change places in the short line-up indicating that a little competition is not necessarily frowned on by the Amish (Ammon, 1994). A pursuit of conceptual or abstract thinking is not promoted in the classroom. There is no "why did this happen?" or "Why do we have to do this?" kind of question asked even at the eighth grade level, unless the accepted answer reflects carefully memorized lists of reasons. National tests of academic achievement pertaining to the elementary grades indicate that Amish children frequently score at a higher average than American children generally, in the subjects which they are taught, even though intelligence tests show Amish children to score at several points lower on the average (Hostetler and Huntington, 1971). This is a standard case that helps to establish that the intelligence test is a measure of cultural absorption more than one of calculating intellectual potential. In any event, it is obvious that the constant drilling of factual data helps Amish pupils to do well on achievement tests, thereby weakening the case of anyone desiring to close down Amish schools on academic grounds.

One of the activities Amish children like to engage in is singing. In one particular classroom, visited by one of the authors, the teacher employed a hymnal printed in Moundridge, Kansas, by the Church of God in Christ, Mennonite (Holdeman) Church. Some Holdeman schools in Alberta, either by design or coincidence, have used Amish-printed materials in their private schools suggesting a case of conservative Anabaptist ecumenicity. Amish children sing lustily and, as the author observed, in two-part harmony, an activity not usually approved by the Amish church. The teacher keeps time with the nod of her head and the end of each line of the hymn is held a little longer than the written music warrants. Also, the teacher sings the first two or three words of the song with the class chiming in as the song gets underway. Perhaps this habit is derived form the ancient concept of the "Vorsinger" (lining the hymn) practiced by some Russian Mennonite groups. Early American religious groups also used this method in days before printed hymnals abounded.

Children are children everywhere, and when the Amish teacher rings the bell for lunch, thirty youngsters clamor around her in search of their brightly colored lunch pails. The contents are gobbled down in less than five minutes so that maximum time can be spent out of doors playing a variety of familiar games. An occasional schoolyard spat, requiring the intervention of the teacher, is a good indicator that human nature is constant regardless of the cultural garb one may wish to dress it in.

Amish schools may be considered a logical extension of home life since the atmosphere is the same as that of the home—authority, respect for the Scriptures and the learning of similar content are all part of the scene. Since the Bible is not available in Pennsylvania Dutch, all fourth graders through eighth graders must be taught High German in order to help them handle the Scriptures (Warner and Denlinger, 1969). The result is that Amish children soon become trilingual: Pennsylvania Dutch for home life, High German for Church, and English for the outside world. Since the school and society generally are English-inclined, it may be that this language is or will soon become the mainstay language of the Amish.

When the members of the Supreme Court of The United States brought down their 1972 verdict in favor of the Amish, the implications of the decision provoked a great deal of criticism and analysis. This decision was deemed significant, not by what it said about Amish schools but what it suggested by implication about public schooling. If education is important to the way of life of the Amish, is it similarly considered by general society? Are the Amish, by this decision to be recognized as a society within a society, separate from what might be called the American way of life? Are they indeed a commonwealth as Hostetler (1993) has suggested?

Today in the more than twenty states where Amish dwell, there are many one-room schoolhouses in operation, run by Amish people. In Waterloo County, Ontario, a similar scenario prevails. Although not legal by provincial law, the provincial government has consistently "looked the other way" with regard to the operation of Amish schools.

Analysis

The successful juxtaposing of at least two significant elements of social functioning such as those presented may be indicative of the endurance of Amish society. If every additional contradiction or dysfunction can be as effectively managed, the future of Old Order Amish may be as assuredly guaranteed as its 300-year-old past. However, there is still at least another consideration.

It may be a somewhat pessimistic view to suggest that internal problems may eventually bring about the demise of the Amish, but they seem to have better success in battling outside institutions than they do with regard to internal struggles. In a long-lasting debate among three academics, Boldt, Frideres, and Peter, the possible demise of the Hutterites (a sister culture to the Amish), has been a point of contention. Frideres (1972) initially argued that a demise is occurring and supported his case by pointing out that there have been systematic programs of discrimination against Hutterites by certain provincial governments in Canada. Peter (1980a) entered the fray to contend that the high birth rate of the Hutterites posed a much more serious threat than that of the Amish. That claim was debunked by Boldt and Roberts (1980) showing that the Hutterite birthrate is declining substantially. Boldt and Roberts maintain that the major threat to the Hutterite way of life is an internal one. Boldt later explicated the claim and Peter (1980b) offered a rejoinder.

Following Boldt's argument, evidence may be examined that reveals that Hutterites have an ever-increasing infatuation with the outside world (Friesen, 1977). It has been observed that there is an increasing rate of defection, an erosion of values, a lessening of traditional taboos on such items as radio and television, a trend toward less austere home furnishings, and more frequent trips to the city for other than strictly business purposes. If Boldt's argument can be applied to the Amish as well as the Hutterites some might argue that the dysfunctional element of these cultural groups is the weakening of their hallowed Anabaptist fervor for social isolation (Peter, 1987).

Consider these factors: first, the generation gap, or break in the socialization process of older youth, is significant because its span is significant. Drugs, liquor, and "more worldly" forms of the forbidden are continuing to be a part of Amish youth culture (Hostetler, 1993). Second, there is a slow but gradual acceptance of limited amounts of technology. If a man thinks he really needs a telephone on his farm and he can convince the elders of his need, he may install one in an outhouse-like structure away from his yard. Naturally, his neighbors will also have access to it. Many Amish also make extensive trips across the United States in rented automobiles driven by their Mennonite neighbors. This provides them with plenty of opportunities to witness the operations of society on a wider scale. No doubt they are at least a little influenced by it. Third, the practice of shunning is growing milder. At one time, Amish girls employed as waitresses were not supposed to serve excommunicated customers even though they worked for non-Amish employers. Now they are allowed to wait on excommunicated members provided they do not directly hand items to such customers or touch them at the same time as the excommunicated person does. Traditionally, Amish people were not supposed to travel in cars with excommunicated individuals even if offered a ride to work by the latter. Today a ride would not necessarily be refused although the orthodox person might make a comment at the beginning of the ride like, "You know I should not be riding with you."

The fourth and final consideration is the lessening fear that the Amish show toward the more liberal elements of the Anabaptist tradition. Friendliness and neighborliness are practiced concepts amid a slightly wider and more diverse circle of contacts. As the Amish grow wealthier they tend to spend money on luxury activities like attending big league baseball games. They also tend to build larger homes with slightly improved conveniences. In Pennsylvania the church is pooling money to assist young farmers to buy high-priced land for farming. The fact that land is much in demand has forced the Amish to increase their wealth as a means of being able to afford to buy land for the next generation. While these developments are not occurring on a grand enough scale to warrant a title brandishing the terms "death of a culture" as Boldt chose, together they may constitute the single most important dysfunctional element of them all, namely, the whittling away of a structure through its own gradually-shifting process (Gans, 1979). As Kraybill has said,

> The future is very uncertain in my judgment . . . I think the urban-suburban culture of this area is a fundamental threat to traditional Amish values. At the heart of the threat are the twin evils always facing the separatism culture: modernism and money. Both are creeping more and more into the church (Klimuska, 1993, A10).

It is sometimes difficult even for the casual observer of culture to avoid commenting on what seems to be an obvious paradox within a given system. What is even more difficult, however, is to be certain that one's assessments and/or analysis of a given situation are accurate, relevant, or even wanted. To be on the safe side, it is probably much better to be a student of culture in the sense of seeking to understand rather than running the risk of engaging in the role of the unwelcome commentator.

Amish culture will undoubtedly endure into the next century, perhaps well beyond that point, but its format will likely change. One of the contributing factors to growth is the high birth rate of the community, and another is the successful transformation the society has made in their vocational theme—from agriculture to cottage craft industries. This shift, however, means that the Amish community of the twenty-first century will only partially reflect the nature of contemporary Amish society. Amish *do* adapt and they *do* change, albeit sometimes reluctantly. What remains to be identified is whether their resistance to change is motivated by strong religious principles or by the fact that they are not too concerned about the nature of change—so long as they lag behind the habits and practices of dominant society to some degree. This concept of relative deprivation appears to be a significant governing principle in determining Amish attitudes toward new phenomena. Change per se is not the issue, nor is it to be feared. What *is* important is for the community to remain somewhat "behind" the developments of dominant society.

References

Ammon, Richard. (1994). Observation of a First-Year Amish Teacher. *Multicultural Education Journal*, 12:2, 6–10.

Beachy, E. R. (1992). *The Plain People: Tales and Truths About Amish Life*. Harrisburg, PA: Stackpole Books.

Boldt, Edward D. (Winter 1980). The Death of Hutterite Culture: An Alternative Interpretation. *Phylon*, 41:4, 390–395.

Boldt, Edward D. and Lance W. Roberts. (1980). The Decline of Hutterite Population Growth: Causes and Consequences—Comment. *Canadian Ethnic Studies*, 12:3, 111–117.

Bryer, Kathleen B. (March 1979). The Amish Way of Death. *American Psychologist*, 34: 255–261.

Durkheim, Emile. (1933). *The Division of Labor in Society*. (originally published in 1893). New York: Free Press.

Erickson, Donald A. (1975). Showdown at an Amish Schoolhouse. *Compulsory Education and the Amish: The Right Not To Be Modern*. Albert N. Keim, ed. Boston, MA: Beacon Press, 84–92.

Fisher, Gideon L. (1978). *Farm Life and Its Changes*. Gordonville, PA: Pequea Publishers.

Fisher, Sara E. and Rachel K. Stahl. (1986). *The Amish School*. Intercourse, PA: Good Books.

Frideres, James S. (September 1972). The Death of a Hutterite Culture. *Phylon* 33: 260–265.

Friesen, John W. (1977). *People, Culture, and Learning*. Calgary, AB: Detselig.

Friesen, John W. (1983). *Schools with a Purpose*. Calgary, AB: Detselig.

Friesen, John W. (1985). Appreciating Cultural Diversity: A Case Study of the Amish. *Multicultural Education Journal*, 3:1, 24–34.

Friesen, John W. Friesen. (1993). *When Cultures Clash: Case Studies in Multiculturalism*. second edition. Calgary, AB: Detselig Enterprises.

Gans, Herbert J. (January 1979). Symbolic Ethnicity: The Future of Ethnic Groups and Cultures in America. *Ethnic and Racial Studies* 2 (1) 1–20.

Guidelines in Regards to the Old Order Amish or Mennonite Parochial Schools, 1978–80. Gordonville, PA: Old Order Amish Steering Committee.

Hagedorn, Robert. (1994). *Sociology*. fifth edition. Toronto: Harcourt Brace & Company.

Henslin, James M. (1993). *Sociology: A Down-to-Earth Approach*. second edition. Boston: Allyn and Bacon.

Hostetler, John A. (1974). *Hutterite Society.* Baltimore, MD: The Johns Hopkins University Press.

Hostetler, John A. (1977). *Amish Life.* Scottdale, PA: Herald Press.

Hostetler, John A. (1980). *Amish Society.* third edition. Baltimore, MD: The Johns Hopkins Press.

Hostetler, John A. (1993). *Amish Society.* fourth edition. Baltimore, MD: The Johns Hopkins Press.

Hostetler, John A. and Gertrude Enders Huntington. (1971). *Children in Amish Society: Socialization and Community Education.* New York: Holt, Rinehart and Winston.

Hostetler, John A. and Gertrude Enders Huntington. (1992). *Amish Children: Education in the Family, School, and Community.* second edition. Fort Worth, TX: Harcourt Brace Jovanovich College Publishers.

Kirkpatrick, Rich. (1981). Amish Barely Tolerate Teenage Car Mania. *Vancouver Sun,* Monday, January 26, 1981, B16.

Klimuska, Ed. (1993). The Amish are Changing. *Lancaster New Era,* July 20, 1993, A10.

Kraybill, Donald B. (1990a). *The Riddle of Amish Culture.* Baltimore, MD: The Johns Hopkins University Press.

Kraybill, Donald B. (1990b). *The Puzzles of Amish Life.* Intercourse, PA: Good Books.

Mennonite Reporter (June 12, 1995). Amish Community Votes to Use Tractors. 25:12, 8.

Marx. Karl. (1906). *Capital: A Critique of Political Economy.* New York: The Modern Library.

Merton, Robert K. (1968). *Social Theory and Social Structure.* New York: Free Press.

Mulkay, M. J. (1971). *Functionalism, Exchange, and Theoretical Strategy.* London: Routledge & Kegan Paul.

Mykrantz, Susan. (1994). Preparing Amish Students for the Adult World. *Holmes Country Traveler,* 6:5, 34–35.

Nagata, Judith Ann. (1968). Continuity and Change Among the Old Order Amish of Illinois. Unpublished Ph. D. dissertation, University of Illinois.

Nolt, Stephen M. (1992). *A History of the Amish.* Intercourse, PA: Good Books.

Peter, Karl A. (1980a). The Decline of Hutterite Population Growth. *Canadian Ethnic Studies,* 12:3, 97–110.

Peter, Karl A. (1980b). Rejoinder to 'The Decline of Hutterite Population Growth': Causes and Consequences. *Canadian Ethnic Studies* 12:3, 118–123.

Peter, Karl A. (1987). *The Dynamics of Hutterite Society: An Analytic Approach.* Edmonton, AB: The University of Alberta Press.

Radcliffe-Brown, A. R. (1957). *A Natural Science of Society.* Glencoe, IL: Free Press.

Redfield, Robert. (1941). *The Folk Culture of Yucatan.* Chicago: University of Chicago Press.

Ruth, John L. (1975). *Conrad Grebel: Son of Zurich.* Scottdale, PA: Herald Press.

Schwartzs' Song Book (1980). Gordonville, PA: Gordonville Print Shop.

Smith, C. Henry. (1957). *The Story of the Mennonites.* fourth edition Newton, KS: Mennonite Publication Office.

Warner, James A. and Donald M. Denlinger. (1969). *The Gentle People.* published by the authors. (n.p.): Galahad Books.

Chapter 6

Perceptions of Amish Music "Unplugged"

Deborah K. Zuercher Friesen

Amish music is probably one of the most neglected areas of Amish literature, yet it comprises an integral aspect of Amish faith and daily living. This chapter reports on an informal study of the important role that music plays in the Amish community.

The German-speaking Mennonites were the largest single group to settle in central Ohio and these people today still form the largest outstanding ethnic and religious community within the state. The Ohio Old Order Amish settlement began in 1807 under the leadership of Jakob Miller (Schreiber, 1962). Ohio has the largest Amish population of any region in the world, with Pennsylvania second and Indiana third. The world's largest Amish community consisting of some 30,000 people is in Ohio Holmes County (Miller, 1992). In this section of Ohio alone there are now more Mennonites than in Switzerland, their country of origin (Miller, 1992).

Research Methodology

In this study four male members of the Amish church and one teenage Amish woman were interviewed regarding music. The one-hour interviews were conducted in person in Amish homes, an Amish bookstore, and at the local livestock auction. All of the interviews were conducted in Wayne County, Ohio.

The Amish music questionnaire used in the study (see chapter appendix) was divided into the following categories: (i) music in daily life activities (ii) music in Sunday worship (iii) music at special community events (iv) music in the Amish parochial school, and, (v) music of the unbaptized Amish youth. The persons interviewed preferred to remain anonymous and did not allow their conversations to be recorded.

Amish Church Types

Three of the four men interviewed are members of different Amish churches. The Ohio Amish live in 216 church districts, each occupying a small geographical area where people can visit each other by horse, bicycle, or on foot. A church district of approximately thirty-five families will meet every other Sunday for worship (Miller, 1992). The 1996 *Ohio Amish Directory* states, "Today, 150 years after the introduction of the Amish culture to this area, there are at least nineteen non-intercommuning church groups which stem from the original congregation" (XIV).

The men interviewed described a continuum of ten different levels of conservatism in the Amish church. Differences in the church types are often subtle and indistinguishable to non-Amish persons. One interviewee, a teenage Amish woman, said that an Amish woman could be distinguished by such features as the number of folds in her head covering or the length of her dresses.

"Type one" churches were identified as the Old Order or "Swartzentruber" type Amish churches. "Swartzentruber" churches have older, stricter bishops and remain the most conservative. "Swartzentruber" Amish refuse to use conveniences such as graveled lanes and were traditionally forbidden by the *Ordnung* to use safety reflectors or lights on their buggies. On the opposite end of the continuum are "type ten" Old Order Amish churches which are the most progressive. The men interviewed each described their church as being a type ten Amish church.

The men agreed that musical activity remained fairly consistent throughout all ten levels of Amish churches, with a few exceptions. More conservative "Swartzentruber" churches never sing in English, do not sing at funerals, and never sing "gospel" songs at social gatherings.

Music in Daily Life

Men are likely to sing hymns in the German language while working alone. This is done as a form of personal spiritual meditation. One man remarked that he practices the new hymns for the Sunday service while he is working. He jokingly added that he tends to hum or sing the words of the "last song he heard" which may be a "country and western" tune that was on the truck radio while being driven to the work site.

Parenthetically, the Amish faith does not allow church members to drive automobiles, although rules vary from church to church on specific transportation details. In many Amish churches, members may own their own vehicles but must hire drivers. They may also travel taxi-style in other driver's vehicles. Some churches do not permit unbaptized teenagers to drive for family members, but will allow the teens to drive for non-related Amish church members. Most Amish people pay approximately $.50 per mile for transportation, regardless of the number of persons traveling in the vehicle. Surprisingly, at least to outsiders, Amish travel for leisure and vacation more than would be expected. It is acceptable to travel by car, motor home, bus, or train if "someone else" does the driving. Travel by air is only permitted in emergency situations.

Amish may also sing as a family in the home. The Amish church does not prescribe a procedure for singing in the home, so the practice varies from family to family. One of the male interviewees has incorporated hymn singing into his evening family devotions. During this informal time, hymns are sung in German or English. Hymns are selected from the *Ausbund*, the *Lieder Sammlung*, *Gospel Favorites* English hymnals, or from memory. "Lamp Lighting Time in the Valley", "How Great Thou Art", and "Come and Dine" were specifically cited as examples of gospel songs that are often requested by the children at family "singings".

When questioned as to how the Amish came to know the melodies to these gospel songs, the men had no definite answer. One man commented that the songs may have been sung in Amish school or heard on the radio. He also recalls hearing his mother sing some of the gospel songs in the home.

Instruments are not allowed to be used by Amish church members. *The Truth in Word and Work: A Statement of Faith by Ministers and Brethren of Amish Churches of Holmes Co., Ohio, and Related Areas* (1983, 43) makes this doctrinal statement regarding instrumental music:

> In the Old Testament dispensation the sounds of instruments and strings were often employed to make a joyful noise unto the Lord. At that time worship emphasized outward ritual. That is no longer what God desires. God desires the expression of our spirit with joy and praise, "God . . . is Lord of heaven and earth . . . Neither is worshipped with men's hands, as though he needed any thing . . . " (Acts 17:24, 25). For when we sing, we are to sing with the spirit and with the understanding also (I Cor. 14:15). Jesus said, " . . . the hour cometh, and now is, when the true worshippers shall worship the Father in spirit and in truth: for the Father seeketh such to worship him" (John 4:23). There is neither spirit nor truth in any musical instrument; therefore the Christian has no use for them. "By him therefore let us offer the sacrifice of praise to God continually, that is, the fruit of our lips, giving thanks to his name" (Hebrews 13:15).

In the Amish home where one interview was conducted, there was a battery-operated electronic keyboard which was used as a "toy" by the children. The man mentioned that "some churches would not allow this". When asked if any Amish children take instrumental music lessons, the man replied that it would be rare, but maybe "one in a thousand" would learn to play an instrument either through lessons or by ear. Levi Miller (1992) states, "Some Amish youth are excellent banjo, fiddle, and guitar players but they give up this entertainment when they join the church in their late teens or early twenties" (24). One Amish man remarked that in the past, Amish teenage "bands" have developed. One such Ohio group, "The Green Tin" (named after a type of beer can) was quite active in performing country/bluegrass/gospel concerts in the seventies and early eighties. The men were not aware of any current Ohio Amish bands but they thought that there may be an Amish teenage band in Indiana.

Amish Worship Music

The primary hymnal used in Amish worship services is the *Ausbund*. The title of the *Ausbund* translates:

> . . . a few beautiful Christian songs as they were now and then made in the prison in Passau in the castle by Swiss Brethren and a few other orthodox Christians. To each and every Christian, of whatever religion, impartially and useful. Besides an appendix of six songs. 13. edition. Published by the Amish districts in Lancaster County, Pennsylvania, 1955 (Schreiber, 1962, 136).

The earliest complete, dated edition seems to be that of 1583 (Bender, 1929). There is a total of 140 songs in the *Ausbund* with an appendix of six ballads added in the seventeenth century. All of the *Ausbund* hymns are strophic (having stanzas). It is rare for the Amish to sing all of the lines and stanzas of these hymns because of the extensive length of the stanzas and the slow tempo in which the Amish traditionally sing these hymns. Paul Yoder states,

> The longest of these *Ausbund* hymns contains 35 stanzas of 13 lines each. Another contains 43 stanzas of nine lines each, and a third is made up of 71 four line stanzas. Many of the hymns contain over 25 stanzas of varying length in the different hymns (Bender, Graber, Springer and Yoder, 1964, 7).

The Amish also use *Lieder Sammlung* which they call "Das Dunne Buchlein" (a thinner hymn book) in Sunday worship services. The preface states that most of the hymns are familiar ones and that the book is of convenient size to carry to services so that each person may have the opportunity to join in the singing. Out of 125 hymns in the first edition of the *Lieder Sammlung*, 43 are from the *Ausbund*. In 1892, S. D. Guengerich, an Old Order Amish layman, published a revised edition containing 70 hymns from the *Ausbund* (Bender, et al.,1964). Reprints of both editions are still available and are used by the Old Order Amish in informal singing, special gatherings, and in the regular Sunday morning worship. The men were uncertain why the *Lieder Sammlung* hymn book is used in their worship services but suggest that it is chosen for practical reasons. The "thinner" hymn book is easier to pack on the "benchwagon" which transports the church pews and songbooks from Sunday to Sunday. *Lieder Sammlung* is also less expensive to purchase.

Neither the *Ausbund* nor the *Lieder Sammlung* have printed music with the hymn texts. The suggestion of a tune name is given at the beginning of each hymn. Paul Yoder counted 82 different tune names mentioned for the total 140 *Ausbund* hymns (Bender, et al., 1964). Because these tunes have been passed down aurally and by rote from generation to generation, there is a great deal of melodic variation from church to church. In 1942 Joseph W. Yoder published *Amish Lieder*; a collection of hymn melodies which he notated from the actual singing of an Amish song leader. The Amish, however, do not sing from Yoder's *Amish Lieder*. The interviewees mentioned that a song book entitled *Nota Buch* is currently used to assist them in singing the pitches of the hymns from the *Ausbund* and *Lieder Sammlung*. The *Nota Buch* is used primarily by men when they meet every other Friday evening for singing practice. Figure 6-1 illustrates the melismatic format of *Nota Buch* notations of hymn texts.

The texts of the *Ausbund* songs are printed in German. William Schreiber (1962) states,

> The hymns of the Ausbund cannot serve as models of correct German. A comparison between the latest American edition of 1955 and an early seventeenth-century copy reveals that the language of the *Ausbund* has not kept pace with the progress which Modern High German has made since that time. Many editors have worked on intermediate editions, but the revisers of even the recent American edition were neither poets nor philologists. The

Ausbund is now neither pure sixteenth century nor pure twentieth-century German, the present edition of the hymnal contains amazing and fascinating mixtures comparable with no other current book. A totally new, or at least different, language has evolved (141).

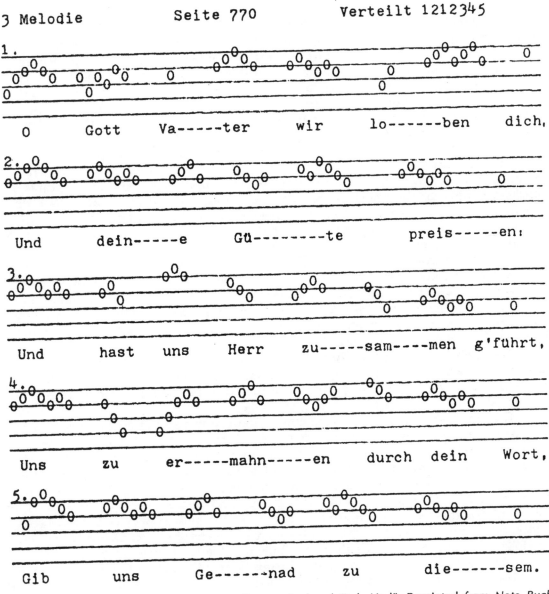

Figure 6-1. *Nota Buch*, Hymn Corresponding to *Ausbund* "Lob Lied". Reprinted from *Nota Buch*. (1990, 15).

Amish church is held every other Sunday. The service takes place in the homes of the Amish church members on a rotational basis. The men attend "singings" every other Friday evening to prepare the hymns for the upcoming Sunday worship service. Women and children may also attend the Friday evening hymn rehearsal, but are not permitted to sing with the men. The women usually "visit" and the children play in another room, while the men practice singing *Ausbund* hymns. No instruments are used to assist with pitch identification.

The men state that the Amish church does not have a specific "Vorganger" song-leader. Usually the oldest church member will begin one song and then nod to the other male chorus members to take turns starting the other hymns. If Amish visitors are present at the Sunday church service, the visitors will be invited to begin the hymn singing. The men and the male children sit on one side of the meeting room and the women, infants and young girls sit on the other side of the meeting room. The men lead in the singing of the hymns at the Sunday worship service, but the women and children have permission to sing along if they know the hymns.

The hymns and scripture for each worship service are preselected and are printed in a calendar entitled the Amish *Register*. The Amish church calendar is correlated with nature's cycle of the seasons. Hostetler (1993) states that the register of Scriptures and *Ausbund* hymns for the Amish church year begins at Christmas time with the birth of Christ and concludes with the New Testament account of the judgment and end of the world (Hostetler, 1963). The *Register* may be purchased for $.25 at Amish book stores. Figure 6-2 illustrates the format of the Amish *Register*.

Selected stanzas from an average of four to five hymns are sung at each service. The worship service opens and closes with the singing of hymns. Individual churches will generally select two or three extra hymns in addition to the ones outlined in the *Register* to "fill more time" while waiting for the ministers to prepare themselves to deliver the sermons and scripture readings. The order of the worship service remains constant from Sunday to Sunday.

The "Lob Lied", on page 770 of the *Ausbund*, is sung at each service. This may be the only *Ausbund* hymn that is sung in its entirety during the worship service. This hymn is described as the "Love Song" and is considered to be the most important hymn of the Amish faith.

The Amish sing their hymns very slowly. Conservative groups sing even slower than progressive groups. Hostetler (1993) writes, "Amish music reflects culture, and the speed of singing can be positively correlated with the rate of the community's assimilation" (230). Among the various Amish groups in Holmes County, Ohio, "Lob Lied" may take as long as twenty-five minutes or as little as thirteen minutes to sing (Scott, 1988). In this prayer hymn, the congregation prays that they may receive God's grace to receive admonition from His Word, and that those who preach may be enabled to rightly speak God's Word. Leonard Clock, the author of "Lob Lied", was a Mennonite preacher in north Germany who came to Holland around 1590. Clock's chief contribution to the Anabaptist churches in Germany and in the Netherlands was his writing of hymns both in Dutch and German (Fretz, 1987).

The first English translation of "Lob Lied"; was set to the tune "Aus tiefer Not" originally recommended in the *Ausbund*. As a result of the many embellishments which

Ein Register von Schriften und Liedern
Die in den Alt-Amischen Gemein-
den gebraucht werden.

Anzufangen am Christtag.

Erster Sonntag.
Schrift: Lucas, 1 und 2.
Lieder: Seite 385, 770, 591 B. 14.

Zweiter Sonntag.
Schrift: Matthäus, 2 und 3.
Lieder: Seite 604, 770, 481, 716 B. 14.

Dritter Sonntag.
Schrift: Matthäus, 4 und 5.
Lieder: Seite 623, 770, 802.

Vierter Sonntag.
Schrift: Matthäus, 6 und 7.
Lieder: Seite 563, 770, 404 B. 17.

Fünfter Sonntag.
Schrift: Matthäus, 8 und 9.
Lieder: Seite 512, 770, (512—11)

Sechster Sotnnag.
Schrift: Matthäus, ·10 und 11.
Lieder: Seite 46, 770, 205 B. 6, 683 B.9.

Siebenter Sonntag.
Schrift: Matthäus, 12 und 14.
Lieder: Seite 316, 770, 278 B. 11.

Figure 6-2. The format of the Amish *Register*.

the tune has acquired through generations of aural transmission, the Amish "Aus tiefer Not" tune is not easily recognized today as being the same tune as the original "Aus tiefer Not" (Fretz, 1987, 24).

The male interviewees cited hymn 492 and hymn 393 in the *Ausbund* as their favorite hymn selections. Hymn 393 was selected because it had an appealing "peppy, Swiss" tune. Hymn 492 was a favorite because of its textual meaning. The men estimate that they know twenty to forty of the *Ausbund* hymns. The teenage Amish woman interviewee confessed that she did not know many of the *Ausbund* songs and she struggled to understand the German texts. She added that she reads the Bible in English rather than in German. She referred the interviewer to speak to her father about the *Ausbund* hymns because he regularly attends the singing practices and has learned the hymns.

The men stated that they learned the tunes and the texts to the *Ausbund* hymns later in life, after they had married and joined the church. Hymns may also have been learned from elders at home and from teachers at Amish parochial schools.

The men all agreed that it was important to have the next generation learn the *Ausbund* hymns. The men tend to believe that the children will come to know the songs when they mature and become church members, as they themselves did. No conscious effort is being made to teach the hymns to the next generation as a means of cultural preservation. However, the men try to make the singing rehearsals a fun fellowship time to attract the younger men to join in. In addition, these men have decided to send their children to the Amish parochial school which will assist in the teaching of the hymns and the German language. The men also believe that the home is a valuable place of learning the German songs and language and voiced regret that they have not done even more singing at home with their families.

Amish Music at Special Community Events

The Amish Wedding is the most festive Amish community event. There are no vocal solos, ensembles, or instrumental songs at Amish weddings. However, group hymn singing is an important part of the wedding ceremony and festivities. There are selected stanzas from three to four hymns which are sung at an Amish wedding ceremony. The "Lob Lied" is always the second hymn of the wedding ceremony.

Informal group singing takes place in the afternoon and evening. Following the noon wedding meal, the men will sing for two to three hours while the women "clean-up". This period of male hymn singing is casual in nature. The men drift in and out of the meeting room engaging in both conversation and song. The young people are usually invited to an evening "frolic" or "singing" on wedding days. Levi Miller (1992) states that on wedding evenings the young people go to the barn for party games, folk dancing, and music.

The Amish funeral service, by contrast, traditionally had no singing at all. Progressive Old Order Amish churches have recently begun to sing one hymn, "Grab Lied" (the "grave song") on page 189 of the *Lieder Sammlung*. This hymn is "lined" at the grave site following the funeral service. The performance practice of "lined" hymn singing includes the bishop reading two lines of text followed by ten to twelve of the male chorus members singing the same two lines of text. One of the progressive Amish churches also added the singing of one hymn during the viewing of the body in the home of the deceased.

The Amish do not sing at other community gatherings such as "barn-raisings" and quilting circles. Hymn singing is not considered appropriate at these work events. However, New Year's Eve is a time of great singing in the Amish community. The congregation gathers in a home around 8:00 p.m. and sings and converses until midnight. Men, women, and children all sing together at this event. Women may start or lead a New Year's Eve hymn. One man stated,

> As it gets later, we start to sing more of the English words and select Gospel hymns from various English songbooks. We also like to sing the traditional German song texts to new melodies such as "Come and Dine" and "How Great Thou Art".

The arrival of the New Year used to be celebrated by sharing a large communal supper of sauerkraut and mashed potatoes but more recently the women have discontinued this practice because it is too much work.

Music in the Amish Parochial School

The first Amish parochial schools originated in Wayne County, Ohio, in 1944 as a result of difficulties between the Amish and the Board of Education. Two court trials were held in the fall of 1944, which charged Amish fathers with violating the 1921 Bing Law requiring compulsory public school attendance of children to the age of sixteen. The presiding judge dismissed the charges.

The Amish parochial school movement grew slowly at first, but by 1958 there were six Amish parochial schools in Wayne County and six in Holmes County. Amish provide an alternative to the pressures of large public schools. Issues that concern the Amish are the use of computers and video technology, organized sports as curriculum, length of school term, Halloween parties, and other activities that conflict with either their cultural or spiritual beliefs (*Ohio Amish Directory*, 1996). By 1994 there were 112 Amish parochial schools in Wayne and Holmes counties with an enrollment of 3,335 students. In the United States there are approximately 848 Amish parochial schools, enrolling nearly 24,000 students (*Ohio Amish Directory*, 1996, XV).

Amish children sing in German and in English at the Amish parochial school. German hymns are usually selected from a special hymnbook called the *Unpartheyisches Gesang-Buch*. Generally two or three hymns are sung in the morning and a prayer is sung at the noon meal. The schools present an annual Christmas program which includes the singing of both German and English Christmas songs from memory. Parents will join with the children in singing Christmas songs. Group singing also occurs on the last day of school to recognize graduates.

Parent/teacher meetings are held once a month to discuss curriculum, problems, and needs of the school. These Parent/teacher meetings open with the singing of two songs and close with the singing of one song. A printed set of standards and require-ments exists for the Amish parochial schools to follow, but aside from these guidelines, each school is operated quite independently.

German classes are taught one to two days a week beginning in the third or the fourth grade. Interestingly, proficiency of the English language is encouraged in the Amish parochial school. In fact, the Amish children are only allowed to speak German at recess on Friday, the one German class day of the week. The following Amish school poem (Fisher and Stahl, 1986, 26) is a commentary on the emphasis that is placed on learning the English language:

ENGLISH PLEASE!

English, English, that's the language
We must speak each day at school,
If instead we speak in German
Then we disobey our rule.

German speech is fine for home-folks,
All the family's gathered 'round;
But at school we must speak English
So we meet on common ground.

Using English daily helps us
With our reading, writing skills.
So come on! Let's all speak English!
We can if we really will.
—Esther Horst

(Fisher and Stahl, 1986, 26). Printed with permission.

Music Practices of Unbaptized Amish Teenagers

The Amish faith exempts youth from obeying the same code of behavior which adult church members choose to follow. Levi Miller (1992) describes Ohio Amish youth activity:

> The Amish allow an informal time of experimentation for youth between approximately fifteen and twenty two or marriage. Some youth will help in charitable mission projects while others engage in rowdiness, drink exces-sively, or frequent country and western music concerts (38–39).

Amish teens from progressive Old Order Churches may own and play musical instru-ments and have radios in their bedrooms.

Two Ohio Amish teenagers reported that Radio WQKT "country western" music was the favorite station among their peers. Artists such as "Alabama" and "Garth Brooks" were cited as examples of performers that are popular with the Amish youth. The Amish fathers interviewed also listed "country and western" music as their children's favorite type of music.

The researcher was curious how adult church members were able to "avoid" overhearing the music of the teens from their bedrooms in the home. One father stated that the radios were not allowed to be used in the main rooms of the house but that he was able to hear the music nonetheless. He did not feel that if he occasionally heard popular radio music that he would be "lost". He added that he has chosen to deny himself luxuries of the world because of his loyalty to Christ and desire to serve Christ in the most righteous manner, according to the teachings found in the Scriptures. Physically adhering to doctrinal legalism against listening to the radio did not seem to be as crucial as maintaining the attitudinal desire to remain separate from the world.

The Amish teens hold group "singings" on the Sunday evenings following church. The young women generally congregate on one side of a table or room opposite from the young men. These teenage "singings" begin around 7:30 p.m. and last for approximately two hours. The hymn selections are chosen from the thinner German hymnal *Lieder Sammlung* or from gospel favorite-type English hymn books. The youth sing the hymns at a faster tempo at their gatherings than in church. The youth may also sing the traditional German hymn texts to other popular gospel melodies. Hostetler (1993) describes deviant youth behavior at some of the more extreme Sunday night "singings":

> The consumption of alcohol has reached intemperate proportions among some of the gangs. "Hoedowns . . . are not hoedowns unless you have music and beer, and a dance every Sunday night after the singing," said one participant . . . The traditional harmonica and guitars have been displaced by electric guitars and transistor-operated tape recorders. At the urging of parents who have lost control over their teenagers, the police have occasionally conducted raids on Sunday night singings.

> Most "hops" are arranged without the consent of the parents . . . After a barn floor holding 150 persons collapsed, injuring several people, the church enjoined parents from allowing parties on their farms. Although the frequency of the "hops" has declined, they have not stopped (356–357).

Hostetler (1993) adds, "Many of the small or moderate-sized Amish settlements do not experience such rowdyism or gang behavior, and it would be unfair to attribute such problems to all Amish" (357). The involvement of the Wayne County, Ohio youth in this type of deviant behavior was not discussed in these interviews. Nonetheless, these "singings" are well attended insomuch as the "singings" are also the primary opportunity for Amish courtship. The young Amish women are offered rides home by interested young Amish men. Most Amish couples' courtships begin at Sunday evening youth "singings" or wedding frolics. Amish teens may also attend secular and religious music concerts and movies before joining the Church.

Conclusion

It has become vogue for rock musicians in the secular world to "unplug" their electric instruments and release recordings of acoustic performances. The Amish do not believe in the use of electricity or instruments so to this extent, Amish music may playfully be described as "unplugged" folk music. The Amish men, during the interviews, repeatedly described singing as a "spiritual" experience for them. It was difficult for them to find other words to define the nature of hymn singing. Hostetler (1993) observes:

> Singing is an integral part of worship for the Amish. For Amish persons, singing evokes the deepest emotions of the human spirit and is thus a source of social unification and group catharsis. No other ritual has such a sustained emotional appeal as does the blending of the individual voice with that of the spiritual community (227).

The dirge-like seriousness of Amish worship hymns parallels the martyr-like lifestyle of the Amish culture. In the *Ausbund*, hymns describing the Christian life as that of a stranger and pilgrim in this world, suffering persecution but loving all men, are dominant (Bender, et al., 1964). The Amish doctrinal statement on singing encourages singing be used only for the edification of the saints:

> Singing is a divine gift of praise and worship. While it is a pleasant, whole-some, and upbuilding activity to be engaged in, it is not intended for mere pleasure, entertainment, or for the gratifying of the senses. Colossians 3:16 encourages that singing be used as a means of edifying or admonishing each other. Special singing for entertainment is not Biblical (*The Truth in Word and Work: A Statement of Faith by Ministers and Brethren of Amish Churches of Holmes Co., Ohio, and Related Areas*, 1983, 42–43).

Although this is the official statement on singing, the Amish seem to make a distinction between singing in worship and informal group singing. Sunday evening, wedding, and family "singings" may serve to edify and admonish the community members, but the music sung at these events is selected increasingly on the basis of the entertainment quality of the music itself. Tempos are increased and new melodies are being learned and adopted. It appears to please church members to sing in this progressive manner.

These preliminary interviews have described the Amish music practices of only three Old Order churches which exist in a close geographical area in Wayne County, Ohio. The Amish persons interviewed provided very similar descriptions of the musical practices of their church districts. It should be noted that the information gained from these interviews was markedly different from the information about Amish and their music described in tourist-literature (see chapter three).

Much of the material circulating about the Amish is outdated, naive, or over-generalized. One of the male interviewee's daughters has a Hutterite penpal and has desired to know more about the Hutterite lifestyle. In order to accommodate this interest the researcher brought two books about the Hutterites to the interview for the family to borrow. When these were handed to the father he simply put them down on the table and said, "If these books about Hutterites are anything like what I have read about the Amish, they won't be true anyway". The daughter was probably not encouraged to read the books.

In music, as in other aspects of life, the Amish probably have their own way of doing things.

References

Ausbund. (1993). Lancaster, PA: Lancaster Press, Inc.

Bender, Elizabeth, Harvey Graber, Nelson Springer, and Paul M. Yoder. (1964). *Four Hundred Years With the Ausbund*. Scottdale, PA: Herald Press.

Bender, Harold. (April, 1929). The First Edition of the Ausbund, *Mennonite Quarterly Review*, III: 147–150.

Fisher, Sara E. and Rachel K. Stahl. (1986). *The Amish School*. Intercourse, PA: Good Books.

Fretz, Clarence Y., ed. (1987). *Anabaptist Hymnal*. Hagerstown, MD: Deutsche Buchhandlung.

Handbook to the Anabaptist Hymnal. (1987). Hagerstown, MD: Deutsche Buchhandlung.

Hostetler, John A. (1963). *Amish Society*. Baltimore: The Johns Hopkins University Press.

Hostetler, John A. (1993). *Amish Society*. Fourth Edition. Baltimore: The Johns Hopkins University Press.

Miller, Levi. (1992). *Our People: The Amish and Mennonites of Ohio*. Scottdale, PA: Herald Press.

Nota Buch. (1990). Funfte Auflage.

Ohio Amish Directory. (1996). Walnut Creek, OH: Carlisle Printing.

Schreiber, William I. (1962). *Our Amish Neighbors*. Wooster, OH: William I. Schreiber.

Scott, Stephen. (1988). *The Amish Wedding and Other Special Occasions of the Old Order Communities*. Intercourse, PA: Good Books.

The Truth in Word and Work: A Statement of Faith by Ministers and Brethren of Amish Churches of Holmes Co., Ohio, and Related Areas. (1983). Sugarcreek, OH: Schlabach Printers.

Suggested Readings

Bartel, Lee. (1986). The Tradition of the Amish in Music. *Hymn*, 37: 20–26.

Bender, Sue. (1989). *Plain and Simple: A Woman's Journey to the Amish*. New York: Harper.

Ein Register. (1995). Baltic, OH: Raber's Book Store.

Hershberger, Alma. (1992). *Amish Women*. Danville, OH: Alma Hershberger.

Jackson, George Pullen. (July 1945). The Strange Music of the Old Order Amish. *The Musical Quarterly*, XXI:3, 275–288.

Korson, George. (1960). *Pennsylvania Songs and Legends*. Baltimore: The Johns Hopkins University Press.

Kraybill, Donald. (1990). *The Puzzles of Amish Life*. Intercourse, PA: Good Books.

Lieder Sammlung. (1993). Lagrange, IN: Pathway Publishers.

Martens, Helen. (1972). The Music of Some Religious Minorities in Canada. *Ethnomusicology*, 16: 360–71.

Smucker, Donovan E. (ed.) (1991). *The Sociology of Canadian Mennonites, Hutterites, and Amish: A Bibliography with Annotations*. second edition. Waterloo, ON: Wilfred Laurier University Press.

Temperly, Nicholas. (1981). The Old Way of Singing: Its Origins and Development. *Journal of the American Musicological Society*, XXXIV:3.

Yoder, Joseph W. (1948). *Amische Lieder*. Huntington, PA: Yoder Publishing Co.

Chapter Appendix
Amish Music Questionnaire

1. Discuss the ways in which music is included in your daily life. For example, Do you sing while working, sing to the children, listen to singing or instrumental music at work or in the home?

2. What is your opinion about listening to music on the radio? On the television? Do you ever attend music concerts? At other churches? At the Relief Sale? Other Mission Auctions? Anywhere else?

3. In Sunday Worship:

   a. How many hymns are sung during the service?
   b. How do the hymns fit into the worship service order? Is the worship service order the same or different from Sunday to Sunday?
   c. How many songs do you know from the *Ausbund*?
   d. How do you learn the *Ausbund* songs? At school, at home, during Sunday worship, chorus practice, or other?
   e. Do you have a favorite hymn selection? Why is this song important to you?
   f. Is there one *Ausbund* song that is the most important to the Amish faith? If so, why?
   g. Beside the *Ausbund*, are there other song books that you use to sing from?
   h. In which language do you generally sing?
   i. Is there a choir or special singing chorus at your church? If yes, when do they practice? Who is allowed to sing in the chorus? What is the procedure during the practice sessions?
   j. Who does most of the singing? The men? The women? The children?
   k. Do you have a song leader? If so, how did that person get chosen to be the song leader? Did he or she receive special training?
   l. Is it important for the next generation to be able to sing the *Ausbund* songs? If so, why? How will the children learn to know these songs?

4. How is music used during important community events such as:

   a. Weddings?
   b. Funerals?
   c. Work times? For example, Barn raisings, quilting sessions?
   d. Other?

5. How is music used in the Amish school?

   a. How is music used during school programs?
   b. In which language do the children sing?
   c. Do you think that it is important for the next generation to know the German language?

    d.   Do you use music to help teach children the German language?

    e.   What is the main purpose for singing in school? Fun social activity for the children? Singing is one way to teach scripture and moral lessons?

6.   What kind of music is allowed for teenagers who have not yet joined the church?

    a.   Are radios, stereos, televisions allowed in the home?

    b.   Are musical instruments like pianos, harmonicas, fiddles, guitars, or keyboards allowed in the home?

    c.   Do the youth attend secular and/or religious concerts?

    d.   What are the teenagers' favorite types of music—rock, country-western, gospel?

Chapter 7

Perceptions of Amish as Deviant

What is Deviance?

To suggest that deviance is in integral part of the Amish way of life is, for some, to suggest the inconceivable. Many aspects of Amish living, such as the emphasis on community and conformity over individuality, the standard ways of dress and behavior, and the similarity of lifestyle, make the Amish appear as a uniform group. Is it not therefore a misnomer to speak about "Amish deviance?"

Well, yes and no. It depends on what is meant by the term "deviance", and whose definition of "deviance" we are using. In its most literal form, the term "deviance" simply means "different from the norm". Although most people usually associate the term "deviance" to connote something bad or evil, by this definition it is obvious that many of us as individuals seek to establish ourselves as different or "deviant" from other people; to develop a unique personal identity which is separate from all others. Deviance, therefore, does not always imply "badness", but simply "differentness".

While human beings generally enjoy seeing themselves as somewhat different than others, most of us enjoy the feeling of being "set apart" from others by virtue of some group affiliation we maintain. We therefore feel special to be included in a group that is, by our own perception, different (or deviant) in some way from other groups. Many enjoy the feeling that comes from perceiving our family, school, religious body, friendship clique, sports team, community or even nation as unique when compared to other similar entities.

While it is possible to see one's group as merely different from others, most people find the temptation to evaluate and moralize overwhelming. In other words, most people in groups divide the world into more than just different types of groups; they also subdivide groups on the basis of their perceived worth. Perhaps it is no surprise to you to find that most of us define the groups of which we are members to be the better, the most moral, or the most superior of all, and other groups to inferior, bad, evil, or wrong.

So if there are two groups coexisting side-by-side, and the members of each group defines their ingroup as the best and the outgroup as wrong, how can you decide which

Figure 7-1. When cultures clash—on the highway.

group is correct? As you can see, it depends very much on one's perspective. In most societies, the opinions of the group with the largest number of members is one whose ideas are defined as normal or "normative", while the smaller group's values are considered "deviant". In these cases the term "deviant" is often applied to the smaller group to do more than just describe; it is an attempt to devalue or discredit them. By doing so the larger group reinforces its feeling of moral superiority and solidarity while discouraging other people from joining the smaller group because of their stigma.

Members of the smaller group, however, often gain something from this relationship as well. With so many people thinking ill of them, this group is bound even closer together with a feeling of uniqueness and a desire to protect one another. Many smaller groups reject the deviant label applied to them, of course; most in fact see the dominant group as the evil empire and themselves as holding onto the better or right way. The fact that most people in the larger society appear to misunderstand those in the smaller group only binds them more tightly together with a grim resolution to survive despite opposition. The forces of evil are understood to be working the hardest against those who are the most right.

One of the authors of this book had the opportunity to interview a man who had engaged in acts of civil disobedience against the United States government during the

1960s. Wanted by the F.B.I. for over 20 years, he had spent most of his life concealing his true identity until he finally gave himself up. He was asked what it was like to spend so much of his life defined as a deviant. His response was, "I saw neither myself nor my companions as deviant. We were simply good American citizens doing our part to take down Nixon's political administration which was deviant, corrupt, immoral and wrong. History bears out which side was right." Despite being a member of a much smaller group, this activist saw the larger and more powerful group as the one who was wrong.

The Amish as Deviant from Mainsteam Society

Since the Amish are a small group in society, they are considered to be deviant or different by most members of mainstream society. Recognize that the point of reference for most evaluators (that is, what is considered to be normal) is what *most* people in society believe and do. When a group such as the Amish develop values and behaviors which are distinguished from those of the larger culture, sociologists refer to such groups as subcultures.

Indeed, Mennonite, Hutterite, and Amish groups were born out of deviance during the Protestant Reformation. During the early 1500s some European governments mandated what religion the people in a geographic area were to be. For Western Europe, this meant Roman Catholicism. During the Reformation, Martin Luther and later John Calvin, were responsible for "converting" entire districts from Catholicism to (what was to become) Lutheranism or the Reformed Church (Calvinism). Still, to choose to believe something other than what the state mandated was to commit the sin of heresy, punishable by death.

There were others, however, who did choose to believe something else. These radicals had been studying the Bible and had come to conclusions very different from those of the Catholic Church or other reformers. Although this was illegal, they met together in a little town called Schleitheim to come to an agreement on principles they had culled from their Bible Study. They were in agreement on the following seven issues:

1. baptism is only for people who confess and follow Christ;
2. members who won't accept the counsel of the church are to be excluded from the fellowship;
3. the Lord's Supper [communion] is to be limited to the baptized, reconciled membership;
4. Christians are to be free of all attachments to non-Christian people and organizations (except marriage, if the other person doesn't leave);
5. pastors are needed for every congregation,
6. force, which may be used by the government, is replaced in the church of Christ by the law of love, which is the only law Christians may use;
7. Christians may not swear oaths (Ruth, 1991, 26–27).

To believe in things such as adult, rather than infant baptism, was deviant enough, but to practice them was all the more so. As a result, these radicals who were called

Anabaptists, meaning "again baptized", were hunted down, tortured, and killed. Michael Sattler, a former monk who likely wrote down the "Schleitheim Confession", had his tongue ripped out of his mouth and was burned to death only three months later. His wife, a former nun, was publicly drowned.

Church and state authorities did not take kindly to Anabaptists, who felt that they were not obliged to follow laws made by the state because, as the Anabaptists claimed, they were accountable only to God and each other, not to any human institution. Despite persecution which continued for two centuries, new leaders emerged. Menno Simons, a former Catholic priest, provided leadership to the group despite being hunted. The group began to be known by the name of this deviant—the "Mennonites". While Menno Simons regularly implemented the practice of shunning the people who sought to live life contrary to the church's teachings, other Mennonite church leaders were less likely to do so. As mentioned in chapter two, in 1693, Jacob Ammann took it upon himself to reinstate the practice within the Mennonite Church, along with foot washing and plain clothing (Hostetler, 1993, 39–40). Thus, the Amish sect was born by deviating from a deviant religious body.

Mainstream Society as Deviant from the Amish

If the idea of considering mainstream society as being deviant from the Amish is amusing, it might be because most of us assume that the group to which we belong is the group which sets the standard for what is normal. In studying subcultures, however, most sociologists, anthropologists and ethnographers seek to understand the subculture from the point of view of the people who are members of it. As a social scientist, the goal is to do so without moralizing or prescribing what should or should not be occurring, and simply describe and explain the *weltangschauung* or worldview of those within the subculture. If one is able to do so, then the Amish community, with its incumbent beliefs, rules, practices and routines becomes the normal way of doing things. To an Amish person, it is mainstream society that is deviating.

Attitude to Change

Over time, and particularly when they emigrated to North America, the Amish came to be seen as more distinct from mainstream society, but this was due more to the fact that society around them was changing at a faster pace than the Amish themselves were willing to change. A statement of faith compiled by ministers and the members of Amish churches of Holmes County, Ohio, states:

> We, the Amish, take a position in our day and society in harmony with that of our heritage. It is more than tradition as many would think. It is the conviction received from an understanding of the Word of God. It is with respect and appreciation that we recognize that our interpretation and application of the Scriptures has remained basically the same for more than 400 years

[sic], though in the face of persecution and adversity *(Amish Brotherhood Publications,* 1983).

Similarly, Miller (1983), a Mennonite, raised in an Amish home, says:

Our people often go up the hill, against the current thinking in our communities. We do it not to be contrary (although we can be stubborn at times) but to be ourselves (5–6).

From an Amish point of view, mainstream society is therefore considered to be moving at a pace which far exceeds the moral dictates of the Bible. To follow the Amish interpretation of Scripture, therefore, is normal; not to follow them is to deviate.

Adhering to the Amish way has often been costly. Besides the hundreds of Anabaptists who lost their lives in Europe simply for believing or practicing something that the state frowned upon, remaining true to pacifist convictions could mean the difference between life and death. One such incident occurred in 1757 in the first organized Amish congregation

Figure 7-2. Parking on market day.

in America near Northkill Creek, Pennsylvania. Jacob Hochstetler, his wife and four children; Jacob, Joseph, Christian and a daughter (unnamed) were asleep in their cabin when their dog made a noise. Joseph Jr. opened the door and was shot in the leg by one of the Native Americans who had been surrounding the house.

Closing and locking the door before the Indians were able to enter, Jacob Jr. and the other two boys reached for their hunting rifles and pleaded with their father to allow them to shoot the eight to ten Indians who were standing in plain sight. The father, a firm believer in non-resistance, would not consent to taking the life of another human being. After their cabin was burned to the ground, the mother, daughter and Jacob Jr. were killed. The others lived with different Indian tribes for several years until the father was able to escape. The sons were later returned due to military pressure on them to do so (Jeschke, 1994).

This incident illustrates how important the ethic of nonviolence is to the Amish. To an outsider, the decision not to fire is fanatic, perhaps even repugnant to some. Yet within the subcultural context, the behavior is thought to be a reasonable Christian response to an unusual situation. To fight back, as the unbaptized sons were wont to do, would have been to act in a deviant manner. Many Amish and Mennonite men were imprisoned, tortured, and even killed in the United States during the Revolutionary War because they refused to harm another human being.

On May 13, 1993, a young driver with no license and no fixed address was driving a Pontiac Lemans down Harrison Road in Holmes County, Ohio at an estimated speed of 65 miles per hour. After passing a truck in a no-passing zone, the driver lost control of the car and smashed into a large group of Amish children who were walking back to their homes from a birthday party. Five Amish children, ranging in age from two to eleven, were killed, and another three seriously injured. A volunteer fire fighter on the scene said "There was crying and hysteria. There were bodies and victims strewn over the area" (Dewey, 1993).

In such circumstances many people in mainstream society would feel obligated to seek some type of restitution or revenge against the perpetrator. In fact, a non-Amish person speaking to Eli Miller, the deacon for the area, said that the driver of the car "ought to be hung". Miller's response was, "Well, that's not the way we feel. . . . We all feel real sorry for him." In speaking with the parents who lost children, Miller said "they all feel the same way. It won't help bring the children back to get mad" (Lewellen, 1993,A4). While the Amish parents and community no doubt grieved, responding in such a way was consistent with the Amish understanding of how they are to believe and act. The driver of the car was eventually sentenced to between seven and fifteen years in prison.

Apparent Contradictions

Further investigation into the complexities of Amish living reveal that, what appears to be contradictory or dysfunctional to outsiders is seen as quite normal or even healthy to members of the Amish faith. Kraybill's (1990) book *The Puzzles of Amish Life* is dedicated to explaining these apparent contradictions. Some outsiders, for example, see the deviance that many unbaptized Amish young people engage in as being rather inconsistent with the Amish practices of avoiding vice, excess, and forbidden material goods such as automobiles. Yet from the Amish perspective, teenage experimentation is a part of the process of making a fully knowledgeable decision to join the church. Since the act of church membership is an awesome commitment, it is good that young people do not enter into such a relationship lightly, but with the full knowledge of what they will be giving up and what they will be gaining. Many Amish parents likewise respect the privacy of their children as they get older, and despite their periodic concern over their childrens' activities parents may not get involved out of a sincere respect for the right of older children to make decisions on their own.

If misunderstanding and disapproval is a reaction of some members of mainstream society to the Amish, it is then understandable when some members of the Amish community react in a similar manner to outsiders. Such reactions can be a rude awakening to tourists who have romantic notions about the Amish way of life. In Wayne County, Ohio, a few Amish men have been observed driving buggies in a manner that does not facilitate the flow of automobile traffic around them even when it is possible for them to do so. "Waving off" the toot of a car horn seems to communicate the idea that, if someone needs accommodating in this situation, maybe the car driver should get a buggy and not be in such a hurry.

Uncomfortable altercations with some members of the Amish community regarding picture-taking appear to be on the rise in Holmes County, Ohio, particularly with tourists. Members of the Amish faith generally dislike having their pictures taken, probably because pictures are vehicles of pride since they are interpreted as being "graven images" forbidden by the Bible. While some Amish will simply ignore picture-takers, others will challenge the apparent invasion of privacy and religion. One tourist, unaware of such religious prohibitions, stopped along the roadside to snap a picture of an Amish man plowing his field. Quickly stopping his team of horses, the man shook his fist at the tourist, kicked dirt into the air and yelled "Stop it—I *hate* you!" Another tourist wanted to take a picture of an Amish school building and waited until the children were inside before pointing the camera at the school. Yet as soon as he did, one of the young boys came running out of the schoolhouse, shaking his fist.

One tourist, desiring to get a picture of some horses, waited patiently until he was sure no Amish person would be in the picture. Raising the camera, he heard yells and whistles as he snapped the picture. "Jackass!" he heard immediately as he lowered his camera. Two Amish men in their 20s approached him angrily and asked, "You got permission to do that?" "To do what?" came the reply. "To take a picture of Amish horses." One of the Amish men smoking a cigarette inhaled deeply. "I'm sorry", the tourist stammered in disbelief, "I wasn't aware I needed permission to take a picture of a horse. Who would I ask for permission?" "Any Amish man around here" the largest man answered, still angry, "'Cause we don't like that!" The tourist was visibly shaken as the two men walked away.

Such confrontations indicate a frustration among some Amish with a larger culture that appears to refuse to respect, accommodate or even conform to the Amish understanding of the world. Similar incidents, of course, have been experienced by the Amish at the hand of non-Amish peoples. These are discussed in a later section.

Amish Communities as Deviant from Each Other

Since the rules in different Amish communities vary, there are times when Amish themselves are not familiar with the definitions of right and wrong in specific communities. The story was relayed to one of the authors of an Amish man who came from a community where it was accepted practice for men to shave until the time that they got married. It was also the practice in this community that, in the rare event that an unmarried man should impregnate the woman he was seeing, he was told to grow his beard in recognition of what he had done. This man traveled to Ohio where it was customary for young unmarried men to grow their beards upon being baptized into the church. It took a few weeks before the visitor gained enough courage to question the moral condition of so many young unmarried men who had to grow beards. He was much relieved to find that the beard indicated baptism rather than pre-marital fatherhood.

Despite many similarities, Amish communities (like other types of religious communities) periodically find themselves in disagreement with each other over issues considered to be of moral importance. Despite the publication of a similar statement of faith (*Amish Brotherhood Publications*, 1983), the 1996 *Ohio Amish Directory of Holmes County and Vicinity* identifies at least nineteen "non-intercommuning" groups which stem from the original congregation.

The splintering of Amish congregations in Lancaster County which was described in an earlier chapter is a process similar in scope to Amish congregations in Ohio; that is, divisions have occurred in both liberal and conservative directions. While several splits have occurred regarding how and when to apply the ban or *Meidung*, divisions have also occurred regarding the use of farming implements, personal appearance, telephones, electricity, Sunday School, and similar issues (*Ohio Amish Directory*, 1996). The decision to splinter a congregation can be painful when family and relatives end up on different sides of the issue, although Atlee Miller says that these differences do not effect the Amish as a community, as neighbors or as friends (Rosenor, 1995).

Social Control in Amish Communities

All societies establish mechanisms for controlling the behavior of their members in order to keep them from straying into deviance. In modern society, the family controls the behavior of very young children, and other institutions like preschools, day care centers, schools, religious organizations, organized sports and the like soon share in both monitoring the behavior of each child and in teaching them the difference between right and wrong. If someone still decides to deviate, the entire legal system, from police to lawyers, judges and prisons, are established to penalize the deviant.

Subcultures and other groups likewise find ways to control the actions of the group. For the most part these mechanisms of behavior control consist of both positive and negative sanctions or rewards and punishments. The Amish and other Anabaptists initially shared a deep concern over monitoring the behavior of church members, since they early on rejected the debauched lifestyles of many members of the state churches, which Anabaptists saw as hypocritical.

Amish Socialization

Many sanctions used by the Amish are also used by other social groups. One of the most powerful tools of social control is called socialization. This means teaching children the cultural beliefs and actions in such a way that they come to believe it on their own. Then, whenever they do what they have been taught to do, they are rewarded internally by a feeling that they have just done something they know to be right and good. Like other social groups, the Amish use socialization as a method of social control. However, unlike mainstream society which depends heavily on the school to do much of the teaching, Amish still depend on the family unit as the primary agent of socialization. It is the family unit that teaches children right from wrong, Biblical values, and all other important qualities of being Amish. This is particularly effective since emotional attachments are also made to other family members. Unlike many teachers, disobeying or disappointing a parent will also bring strong emotions into play, thus making a deviation all the more onerous.

Other Amish institutions help to supplement the socialization children receive at home. The Amish school, described in chapter five, assists in the moral development of each child, as does the church. To the outsider, however, it may be surprising how little these institutions are depended upon for socialization. The Amish fought against a formal system of education of any kind for many years. Education was seen as potentially increasing the pride of an individual in a community which values humility. Only after the compulsory public education system was implemented did Amish people seek to establish their own schools. Even then, Amish children do not go to school beyond grade eight. Similarly, Sunday School in church has been avoided by most of the Amish groups. Lack of exposure to other ideas and a lower amount of formal education, then, serve to insulate Amish children and increase the likelihood of conformity.

The Amish affection for farming and agriculture is also partly an embracing of certain mechanisms of social control. On the family farm, there is much hard work to do, thus reducing the amount of free time where idle hands and minds might otherwise get into trouble. Amish people are not afraid to do work for the sake of work, but will reject some labor-saving devices with the explicit purpose of providing more work for a growing family. In addition to work, the family unit cooperates together to make sure everything gets done. Unlike modern society where one or more parents leave for the better part of the day, supervision of children's activities is greater at all times.

A successful socialization experience culminates in the individual choosing to conform to the strict rules and regulations of the community. This decision is embodied in the act of individual baptism. Like other Anabaptist groups Amish do not practice infant baptism, believing that following Christ should be an individual decision and that this decision be made as a "fully aware" adult. Before baptism Amish youth are not held to the same behavioral standards as baptized members. Besides the religious importance of baptism, then, the choice to become baptized symbolizes an inner desire to conform to the standards of the community and to defer one's own judgment to that of the community. Obedience and humility are expected of all baptized members, and through the act of baptism one openly acknowledges a willingness to be monitored and controlled by the larger Amish community.

Hershberger (1992, 33–35) relates a poignant story which illustrates the difference in expectations among baptized and unbaptized members. A young Amish man left his Amish roots, met a Catholic woman and they were married. Years later the man desired to re-establish himself in the Amish community and his wife agreed to join as well. The Amish bishop agreed and granted the young woman a period of grace for one year in order to be instructed about the Amish traditions and rules. She was invited to receive instruction every other Sunday with the other young Amish boys and girls seeking membership. The man quickly completed his training, was baptized, and began dressing in Amish clothes and growing whiskers. For six months, however, his wife was allowed to drive her red convertible and wear shorts. When she was baptized, she too began dressing in traditional Amish garb.

The Ordnung

The church and the community are inseparable entities in Amish society, and it is this body which provides the broader parameters for acceptable social behavior for the members. Twice a year the local leaders seek the consensus of the community to endorse the *Ordnung* (rules) of their particular fellowship. These rules define acceptable and unacceptable behaviors, thus providing a clear path for those who desire not to deviate. Regarding the *Ordnung*, Schreiber (1962) says: "The Amish . . . are firmly convinced that, the more restrictions and burdens they set upon themselves, the more assured they may be of eternal salvation. These thoughts are the marrow of their preaching" (40).

The *Ordnung* is personified in the man occupying the position of bishop. It is he, in consultation with preachers and deacons, who sets the character of the district and monitors the behavior of its members. Bishops are important mechanisms of social control simply by their gaze, and they embody the rules of the entire community. The power of the bishop is relatively great, and his opinions can effect the future of many peoples' lives within the community. If a member is not living a life acceptable to the *Ordnung* of the Amish community, it is the bishop who begins the implementation of negative sanctions.

During this research Amish friends informed us of special "confessional" services which are held periodically to provide parishioners with an opportunity to confess their sins to one another as per the Biblical injunction found in James 5:16. These meetings give members an opportunity to disclose wrongdoings, be prayed for to seek forgiveness, and to be reconciled to the community once again. In some areas, if a bishop has a suspicion regarding the activities of a particular member and that member does not voluntarily stand up to confess, the bishop will publicly confront the person regarding the alleged activity. If the member acknowledges the sin but does not ask for forgiveness, more serious consequences would be forthcoming. These meetings thus function as another method of maintaining social control, and encourage submission to the community, and obedience to the *Ordnung*.

Physical violence and/or incarceration is a primary method of negative sanctioning used in mainstream society by agents of social control. However, among a peaceable people such as the Amish who abhor violence and physical conflict, what types of negative sanctions (other than confessional services) are used to admonish a straying member? The answer, of course is both the threat and actual use of the *Meidung*, also known as "shunning" or use of the "ban".

In and of itself the application of the *Meidung* is an awesome and terrible experience for the person or family to whom it is applied. Since Amish communities are so close-knit and unique in terms of subcultural behaviors, beliefs and worldview, being ostracized means breaking contact with the people and way of life with whom you have grown up and are related to. The specific application of the ban differs between congregations, but often family members are not allowed to communicate with the banned person, or even to take things from them directly. If the shunned person operates a business, Amish will not be permitted to buy things from the operation and may thus induce bankruptcy.

If the application of the *Meidung* is effective as a means of social control, the fear of the *Meidung* is equally so. Members are much more willing to comply with milder injunctions regarding their behavior because of the enormous perceived social, emotional, spiritual and economic losses. Seldom do behavioral problems get to the stage where the *Meidung* is seriously considered, so effective is the threat of its implementation. However, there are times when people choose to suffer the consequences. During one of the confessional services a young woman stood up and confessed that she had been "fornicating" with her boyfriend, who was also in attendance at the meeting. After praying with her to receive forgiveness, the bishop invited the young man to stand up and confess. Somewhat surprised by the confession of his girlfriend, the young man refused to do so and was eventually excommunicated.

Further evidence of the use of the *Meidung* as a means of social control is the manner in which previously-shunned members are received when seeking forgiveness and reconciliation. No matter how serious the offense, any member will be readily readmitted when willing to admit the error of his or her ways. Instead of being used as a permanent punishment for some embarrassment caused to the community, the *Meidung* is applied as a means of social control in an attempt to get the individual to conform to the wishes of the group.

Deviance as Crime

Thus far this chapter has explored the dimensions of deviance as being *different* than other groups, and the idea that these differences are often evaluated on a moral basis. Deviance also encompasses those behaviors that are criminal in nature. Mainstream society has established a long list of formal rules and regulations known as the *law*. To break the law in North America is to engage in crime, regardless of what subcultural values to which you may adhere. We noted in chapter two the highly unusual case where an Amish man was shunned by his congregation and, since he faced financial insolvency because Amish were not allowed to purchase goods at his store, he sued the bishop and church leaders for a boycott which, he claimed, was illegal. Having been ousted from his church, the Amish parishioner appealed to a "higher authority", the legal system of the United States.

In defining deviance as crime we are referring to those specific behaviors that run counter to the laws of the government which claim control over a particular territory. For most of the Amish today this means the government of the United States, its respective states and municipalities. It is apparent that two types of crime occur in relationship to the Amish—crimes committed by persons of Amish extraction, and crimes committed against the Amish by others.

Crime by Amish

The deviant origins of the Anabaptists, of which the Amish are a part, were noted earlier. In the 16th century it was illegal simply to be an Anabaptist in Europe. Since emigrating to North America, Amish have periodically clashed with government authorities regarding their unwillingness to compromise on issues of principle. Today, the Amish pay taxes, social security and sales tax while refusing to receive any welfare, unemployment, medical or retirement benefits.

While the Amish respect the government and are generally quite law-abiding, Hostetler (1993) notes that at least four issues have caused confrontation between the government and the Amish: (i) consolidation of small elementary schools, (ii) lengthening of the period of school attendance and the subsequent requirement of high-school attendance, (iii) compulsory welfare systems, and (iv) conscription. At times Amish people have been jailed for failing to comply with government ordinances. Some parents were arrested as many as ten times for failing to send their children to Pennsylvania high schools.

Since most baptized Amish individuals respect the law for the most part, few crimes are committed by members of this group. Periodically, however, they may be committed by individuals acting without the approval of the church. In the early 1800s, for example, John Hochstetler and his wife Magdalene were married and lived in Pennsylvania. Magdalene's sister Barbara Lehman had been helping Magdalene with some housework, when they placed the Hochstetler baby into her cradle and went outside to assist John in tapping trees. They returned to the house only to find the baby dead, having been smothered between the parts of another bed.

Barbara claimed to have seen John's brother Solomon around the house, but a jury did not find sufficient information to convict Solomon. It was not until years later that a respected member of the community confessed to the murder when he thought he was dying. He had been deeply in love with Barbara who spurned his love, and this man felt the Hochstetlers had turned Barbara against him. Upon approaching the Hochstetler cabin one day he saw the two women leave the house and thought they were evading him. In anger he killed the baby (Jeschke, 1994).

Equally disconcerting is the story of Eli Stutzman of Ohio, who appears to have killed his pregnant wife and placed her body in his barn to which he subsequently set fire. Due to personal problems, mostly attributed to mental problems, Stutzman took part in drug abuse, violence, and one-night homosexual encounters while traveling across the United States with his young son. At nine years of age the body of Stutzman's son Daniel was found dumped in a Nebraska ditch in a blue sleeper. Dubbing him "little boy blue", the Nebraska community gave him a full funeral before learning that his father had killed him (Olsen, 1990).

Aside from these isolated cases, any crime committed by the Amish is usually committed by adolescent males before they join the church. Since this time is looked at as a period for decision-making, many young people explore the darker side of existence by engaging in recreational activities that are illegal. These include underage drinking, driving without a license, drug use, and similar activities. Unbaptized Amish teenagers periodically get together during or after "singings" and engage in such activity. The parties can grow so loud and boisterous that the parents on whose farm the singing is held may even call the police. The *Philadelphia Inquirer* offered this description:

> A weekend-long end-of-summer hoedown attended by about 500 young Amish in Lancaster County was broken up by police Saturday night after neighbors complained about loud rock music and underage drinking. Police from five small Lancaster County departments descended on Mill Creek at 9:30 p.m. warning the partygoers to clear out or be arrested, according the a West Lampeter police officer. "It was getting uncontrollable, " he said. "We decided to shut it down." . . .

> Many of the Amish men arrived in automobiles, instead of the customary horse-drawn buggies, and wore modern "English clothes" rather than the dark suits and hats approved by the church. Most of the women wore the traditional Amish dresses and bonnets.

> The officer added that the parties were "known for underage drinking," and that there had been arrests in previous years. "This year," he said, "when we went in, the underage kids ran from us" (Kephart and Zellner, 1994, 41).

Crimes Against the Amish

Of much greater frequency and concern than crime committed by the Amish is the amount of hate crimes that are committed *against* the Amish by others. Some people incorrectly believe that the Amish are a drain on the American economic system, while others are irritated at the Amish's stand against military service. Committed to a life of nonviolence and nonresistance, visibly recognized by outsiders, and using slow means of transportation, Amish are easy prey to those who would take advantage of them. Tourists visiting areas heavily-populated by the Amish often do not realize how slow Amish buggies travel and do not anticipate a slow-moving buggy just over the crest of a hill. Amish people and horses are killed or seriously injured almost every year in Holmes County, Ohio, and Lancaster County, Pennsylvania due to motor vehicles smashing into the back of them.

Other people seem to take delight in spooking horses by honking the horn as they pass by, or by cutting in on the horse before the vehicle is fully past. On the shoulder of a busy highway, one of the authors happened upon an Amish woman tightly clutching the bridle of a horse attempting to bolt. A passing vehicle had spooked the horse. It appeared as if the woman were in danger of being trampled by the horse. Several crates of fresh produce had spilled out of the sides and back of the buggy which were clearly destined to be sold at a roadside stand. In a matter of minutes the driver of another vehicle (along with the author) stopped to help. After the horse was calmed and the produce was picked up, the woman proceeded on her way.

Wittmer (1971) has noted that non-Amish resentments and hostility are often expressed towards the Amish in violence and harassment. Kephart and Zellner (1994) note a rash of barn burnings in the Lancaster area in 1992, likely the object of hate crimes for non-Amish arsonists. Amish women have been raped and families have been robbed at gunpoint while in their buggies. In March of 1996 in Wayne County, Ohio, a car slowed down beside a buggy carrying an Amish family, and an occupant of the car demanded the driver of the buggy to stop. Realizing the potential danger the buggy driver continued on, until the car's occupants took shots with a firearm. One of the young boys was shot through the foot; the horse was hit in the leg later had to be put down.

Other people seek to harm or frustrate the Amish seemingly for the purpose of vandalism or exercising control over other people. A Mennonite friend of the Amish was startled one evening by pounding on his front door. An Amish man reported to him that someone had been driving past his buggy while throwing rocks, and that he and his family were scared to proceed down, the less well-traveled road to his home. Rocks can easily pierce the thin canvas wall of the buggy and cause serious injury to its occupants. Following the buggy in his car, the Mennonite man soon saw a car rapidly approach, its occupants throwing rocks at the buggy. In giving chase, he noticed that the young people in the car were those who attended a nearby Mennonite church.

Conclusion

This chapter has discussed the meaning of deviance as simply being different from that of another group. Deciding whether it is the Amish or mainstream society which is deviant depends very much on one's perspective, although the group with the larger number of members is usually considered to be "normative". The Amish deviate in very specific ways from mainstream society, and use very specific (although not unique) methods by which to control their members. With rare exception, baptized Amish are generally law-abiding citizens but they are still frequently the victims of hate crimes. Apparently, North American tolerance still has a ways to go.

References

Amish Brotherhood Publications. (1983). *The Truth in Word and Work.* Sugarcreek, OH: Schlabach Printers.

Dewey, Mike. (1993). "Five Children Killed as Car Goes out of Control", *Wooster Daily Record,* May 14, A2.

Hershberger, Alma. (1992). *Amish Women.* Kalona, IA: Round Table Inc.

Hostetler, John A. (1993). *Amish Society,* fourth edition. Baltimore, MD: The Johns Hopkins University Press.

Jeschke, Betty Miller. (1994). *Amish Pioneers of the Walnut Creek Valley.* Wooster, OH: Atkinson Printing.

Kephart, William and William Zellner. (1994). *Extraordinary Groups: An Examination of Unconventional Life-Styles.* fifth edition. New York: St. Martin's Press.

Kraybill, Donald B. (1990). *The Puzzles of Amish Life.* Intercourse, PA: Good Books.

Lewellen, David. (1993). Amish Deacon: "We're Not Angry at the Guy; We Feel Sorry for Him", *Wooster Daily Record,* May 26, A4.

Miller, Levi. (1983). *Our People: The Amish and Mennonites of Ohio.* Scottdale, PA: Herald Press.

Ohio Amish Directory Holmes County and Vicinity. (1996). Walnut Creek, OH: Carlisle Printing.

Olsen, Greg. (1990). *Abandoned Prayers.* New York: Popular Library.

Philadelphia Inquirer. (1984). Quoted in William Kephart and William Zellner *Extraordinary Groups: An Examination of Unconventional Life-Styles.* fifth edition. New York: St. Martin's Press.

Rosenor, Rhonda. (June, 1995). Amish Orders Set Apart by Biblical Interpretations. *The Amish: A Culture, A Religion, A Way of Life.* Special section in the *Holmes County Hub.*

Ruth, John L. (1991). *The Believers' Church Story.* Elgin, IL: The Brethren Press.

Schreiber, William I. (1962). *Our Amish Neighbors.* Chicago: University of Chicago Press.

Whitmer, Joe. (1971). Cultural Violence and Twentieth Century Progress, *Practical Anthropology,* 18, 146–155.

Chapter 8

Perceptions of Amish Future

The Amish community had a third century birthday in 1993, proving itself to be a fairly stable society. Insofar as the history of civilizations is concerned, however, it will be remain to be seen how successful the Amish are in maintaining their way of life in the face of unprecedented technological development, much of which they are injecting into their way of life. Many civilizations and societies in the past have not even lasted 300 years, while others lasted much longer—and yet shrank into oblivion. Still others have persisted, thrived and endured. The community of First Nations of North America is an excellent example of the latter group. The secret of remaining alive is a mystery, however, and probably varies from one civilization to another. A formula that works for one society may not necessarily work for another. A healthy cultural composition is no guarantee for future endurance. The central challenge seems to be for a culture to be able to endure is for its adherents to learn how to effectively handle its most threatening influence. In the case of the Amish, centered as they are on resisting the use of technology, seems to be just that. More Amish today than ever before are involved to some extent in utilizing some direct form of technology or benefiting from its use in a secondary capacity. Many Amish today also work in small town urban and suburban environments, thereby either coming into contact with technology or having to use some form of it in their work. Some Amish use telephones in business, and others have had to become computer-wise in order to survive. Amish-run businesses, many of which are "cottage industries", now produce virtually every kind of product from A to Z, including the manufacture of farm equipment, furniture, and playground equipment as well as a series of products targeted directly at the tourist market. Amish women have entered the trade with a full range of home-sewn items including quilts, tablecloths, tea-towels, potholders, and even dolls. The opportunities to do well in this kind of economic climate, plus the scarcity of farmland have pulled the Amish off the land by the magnetic force of modernization. In light of these factors it has simply not been possible for the Old Order Amish to maintain a strictly agricultural form of lifestyle. They are now in many ways competitive American business-men, manufacturers, managers and salepersons.

This change in lifestyle has pretty well had to have effected a parallel shift in philosophy, the full extent of which will be realized in the future.

An Agrarian-Based People

The Old Order Amish have basically survived and excelled as farmers for three centuries. Their way of life began on such a model and this appears to have worked well for them because of the limited access this way of life has allowed with the outside world. The Amish interpret the Bible as admonishing an agricultural lifestyle for them, and as with other aspects of their society they believe it necessary that they fulfill to the letter the intent of the scriptures. This farming format of living has also augured well in keeping children from becoming victims of outside influences.

The Lancaster Experience

In Lancaster County, many Amish farms have been in possession of the same family for over a hundred years, a good example of the stability of the community. But today there are new challenges to the family farm. Farm prices are high and land is scarce, and many Amish have found it necessary to seek a living elsewhere. Only about half the farmland in Lancaster County is owned by Amish, and when a farm does become available for sale, even poor land will sell for very high prices. A good farm of sixty acres or more, with good buildings, can bring nearly a million dollars in cash when sold. Amish lands rarely pass out of Amish hands and when "English" lands go on the market they are usually bought up by Amish. Still, there is never enough land to go around and many of the sons of large families have to look to other occupations for a livelihood or seek to establish farms elsewhere. This is very difficult for the Amish to do because they have a long history in the county and they have formed an emotional attachment to the area. A futuristic kind of measure undertaken by the Amish church in Lancaster County has been to purchase land in the name of the church and sell it to young Amish farmers. At the present time the Old Order Church owns about 1,800 of the county's 4,900 farms. This reality threatens to shatter the image of the family farm and places the Amish church squarely into the ranks of the typical American corporation.

In 1940, the population of Lancaster County was about 210,000 and virtually everyone, Amish and non-Amish, was involved in farming. Today, more than 430,000 people live in the county, and only about 18,000 of them are Amish. For the past two decades the county has flourished as an industrial and business center, making virtually every rural area into part of the urban Pennsylvania countryside. Fifty years ago, the Amish "capital" town of Intercourse consisted of two grocery stores, two feed mills, a flour mill, a tinsmith shop, a furniture store, a harness shop, a blacksmith shop, two restaurants, an equipment dealer, a shoe repair shop, a post office, a bank and a few other businesses. Today the town retains its Amish flavor, but Amish-run businesses and tourist outlets have become as numerous and as respectable as traditional Amish farms. Amish population in the Lancaster County has increased by about 15,000 in the last half

Figure 8-1. Shopping day.

century and the Old Order people have become a vital part of the established order. Added revenue from the new branches of business development have enabled the Amish to build more modern homes, and yield to the increasing pressures to add new "frills" to their household schedule and inventory. The fatter income checks are now relegated for vacations to the west coast, trips to Veteran's Stadium in Philadelphia to watch the Phillies, and obtain the latest in shop equipment—lathes, drills, sanders, rip saws, bench saws, jig-saws, and molders (Klimuska, 1993, A1). In the early days of the Anabaptists, persecution bonded them together in the faith; today that very bond is being threatened by wealth and prosperity. No doubt this trend also has its costs in terms of maintaining community, and the factions keep appearing. The most recent split within the Lancaster Community Amish community occurred about thirty years ago and concerned the use of certain farm technology.

A very promising farm-related Amish enterprise in Lancaster County is dairying. The average Amish dairy milks about 40 cows with automated machinery run by a 12-volt electrical system. Amish use automatic suction milkers, have refrigerated bulk tanks, practice artificial insemination and rely on the advice of educated veterinarians to make the most of their operation. Their barns have the latest equipment, and milk is pumped from the cows to bulk tanks in glass pipelines. Cattle are fed scientifically-calculated diets in order to be able to fulfill their potential and produce their maximum milk supply. If all of this sounds miles removed from the "ole country style" of Amish living one reads about in tourist literature, well, it is. Few farmers in America put as much energy and dedication into getting and maintaining maximum production from their cows as the Amish do. They may be driven by the "old time religion" but for them it translates nicely into a made-for-America form of capitalism.

Change Pressures

As the pressures on the traditional Amish lifestyle emanating from the wonderful world of technological development continue to make their impact increasingly ingenious approaches are invented to legitimize changes in the eyes of church leaders. The use of electricity is basically forbidden by most Amish *Ordnung,* but wind power, gasoline-powered engines to provide energy to 12-volt batteries are allowed. Today many Amish businesses simply convert 12-volt electrical systems to the standard 110-volt system in order to be able to operate various modern forms of technology including cash registers and calculators. Amish businessmen argue that without this equipment it would be impossible to compete with non-Amish businesses, so they are "forced to modernize". Others will argue that the addition of Amish industries are essential to keeping their children at home. In any event, the millions of dollars spent annually in Lancaster County by tourists has to be a highly motivating factor for the constant increase in Amish ventures into the sales-to-tourists business.

The Cultural Clash

Legal Clashes

Legal involvements of the Amish with the state have a long history in America. Despite their refusal to have any more to do with secular authority than necessary, the Amish have for a long time been involved in one court case or another, most of them having to do with schooling. In 1937 Amish leaders battled local school authorities who were consolidating small country schools into large centralized districts. This motivated a series of Amish migrations to Lebanon County, Pennsylvania, and Maryland. It was the first exodus of Amish from their favorite county. Later there were migrations to Kentucky, Indiana and other states. By the 1940s a sort of truce had been reached with regard to the school issue and the country's attention was turned to World War II. When the war was over the battle resumed with the Amish gaining permission to operate their own parochial schools. In an attempt to convince government authorities of their sincerity, several Amish bishops travelled to Washington to consult with federal authorities about their longstanding school consolidation problem. Federal authorities resisted, unable or unwilling to appreciate why the operation of parochial schools was so important to the Amish. It was twenty years before the Amish gained supreme court approval to operate these schools.

Figure 8-2. Buggy style—covered style.

Although the Amish try to avoid any and all forms of interaction with government, the development of Amish parochial school centers on their dealings with all levels of government. With the school question settled, a new round of involvements have occurred having to do with zoning laws, planning commissions and mandates from state and federal officials regarding environmental matters, crime, municipal rulings and other factors that impinge on the operation of Amish businesses. The Plain People now have to deal with such matters as location, and in line with which building regulations, to build their homes, how to avoid contaminating country creeks and streams, and how to stay within the rules when starting up new plants and stores. Usually these matters are settled quite peacefully with state officials, with the Amish trying to comply with all regulations. Still, this new kind of involvement continues to bring the Amish closer and closer to the kind of experience that all citizens have with their governments.

Community Reaction

The image of Amish as peaceful, sedentary and humble farmers is not necessarily shared by all of their neighbors. Their non-Amish competitors often see them as aggressive, industrious, hard-nosed businessmen whose acumen may possibly affect their own prosperity. Government officials at all levels—county, state, and federal—view them as American citizens with the same wants, needs and desires as their peers. They want to enjoy the good life on their own terms. When this "normal" desire clashes with the interpretation of how to arrive at the good life as defined by other citizens, some mutual adjustment has to be made. That adjustment is usually explicated in legislation, laws and bylaws. The government bureaucrat's job is simply to enforce them for the good of all.

Community reactions to their Amish neighbors are mixed. Most probably get along with or tolerate them, but there are occasional cases of suspicion, distrust or even competitive jealousy. Seldom does the situation erupt to the status of the event of April, 1992, when seven Amish barns near Harrisburg, Pennsylvania, were burned by vandals for no apparent reason. Six of the barns were totally destroyed and 177 horses and cows were killed in this vicious action. The investigative work by police was made more difficult by the Amish who insisted on rebuilding the barns before the investigating officers had the chance to do their jobs. It takes time for the ashes of a burned-down barn to cool, to the point the officers when the officers are able to sift through the ashes to determine the possible cause of the blaze. Since the Amish carry no insurance they often cannot be bothered with a long wait before rebuilding. While their philosophy towards those who do them wrong is pacifist in objective, reports were that some of the Amish would like to see the perpetrators of the crime punished. The FBI investigated the arson as a possible hate crime involving civil rights violations. Other observers speculated that the barns may have been ignited by a disillusioned excommunicated Amish individual (*People Magazine*, 4/13/92). In any event, the situation has contributed towards a state of uneasiness about neighborly relations among the Amish.

Migrations

When tension arises in an Amish community, caused by either internal or external pressures, at least two options are available—form a new faction or migrate to a new location. At times congregations relocate to more isolated areas that are less exposed to outside influences (Schreiber, 1990). Lancaster County has spawned twenty-three new congregations since 1940 although the Amish population in the county tends to be very stable. Kraybill (1990) reports that nearly two dozen church districts, representing nearly four thousand people can trace their roots back to Lancaster County. There are currently Amish living in twenty-two states and in Ontario, Canada. Migrations outside of North America have never been seriously considered by the Plain People.

Amish migrations occur for a variety of reasons, as Hostetler (1993) points out. The motivations for relocation may have to do with church discipline—either to escape rigidity or to reestablish it, to elude church problems, to avoid industrialization and overcrowding, or simply to obtain affordable land. At times they may even occur for personal reasons such as the lure of the land.

In 1975 a young Amish individual named Steve Kauffman, satisfied his thirst to move west by purchasing a 2,700 acre farm in the West Kootenai area of northern Montana with two partners. The three decided to attempt to establish an Amish colony in the area by selling off small parcels of land (160 acres in size) to friends they might attract from back home. The settlement is located about an hour's drive west and north of Eureka, Montana. Shortly after Kaffman and his colleagues established themselves they were joined by thirty-five families from Ohio who migrated to Montana, leaving their prosperous farms behind. Although it was their intent to farm in the new settlement, weather conditions dictated otherwise. This was primarily ranching country, except for the huge amounts of timber in the area. This motivated the establishment of a lumber mill (Border Lumber) which grew to employ more than two dozen workers. The mill is powered, of course, by a gasoline engine. It employs about 35 people, and offers steady work. Still, the loneliness of being so far away from home proved to be too much for some members of the community and within a decade or so about half of the population returned home to the eastern states. Those who remained built a schoolhouse, a store, a buggy shop and a bed-and-breakfast. A few families raise cattle as a sideline. When the Amish relocate to a new area there is always a concern that the migrating group will include ministers to provide spiritual direction, and someone to handle educational responsibilities. The Montana community had to wait a few years before this objective was realized, but eventually two ministers decided to settle in the community. Various individuals took turns taking charge of schooling and to date more than a dozen different people have served as teachers (Hochstetler, 1991).

The Canadian Experience

After the American Revolution the Canadian Government offered free lands and other inducements to would-be immigrants whose loyalties still lay with the British who controlled Canada (Zook, 1988). The first Amish settlers arrived in Canada in 1822, and after three years a steady stream of Amish immigrants also arrived from Europe. Their counter-parts in Pennsylvania chose Ontario, Canada, as a future home as a result of the Revolutionary War in America making Waterloo Township in Ontario recipient of Amish people from both sources. Most of the Amish who came to Canada were relatively poor, and part of their motivation in migrating was to better themselves. After 1850, a degree of prosperity set it, evident in the larger homes that the Amish built for themselves with a frame construction bolstered by field stone and brick. Internal clashes were triggered by such matters as wearing of beards, women's dress (the wearing of veils over the top of caps was discontinued), to purchase or not to purchase insurance, progressive farming techniques and excessive use of alcohol (Gingerich, 1972). In 1886 the Amish in Canada experienced their first major division when two congregations decided to go their separate ways. Shortly thereafter a number of families left Canada for various American states, partly because of stressful economic conditions and partially to escape the tensions at home. Still the Amish community in Canada has prevailed; it is estimated that nearly three thousand Amish presently live in Ontario (Hostetler, 1993). The Canadian Amish include seventeen districts, all but one of them formed by immigrants from the United States.

The Ontario Amish have developed several subfactions, one of which has adopted a quite "modern outlook" in that members are allowed to participate on government programs such as family allowance, health insurance plans, and old age pension. This conference has even accepted government funds for the erection and operation of some of its community-serving institutions. The leaders still claim to believe strongly in separation of church and state but they also add that this does not mean that the two parties cannot cooperate with one another (Gingerich, 1972). Traditional Amish groups in Ontario have managed to work out an arrangement with the federal government whereby as farmers they are exempt from some government programs under a special classification as "self-employed businesses" (Regehr, 1993). This arrangement did not come easily. In 1967 Revenue Canada officials began to invade Amish bank accounts and garnered wages in an effort to collect unpaid Pension Plan taxes. In 1974 the Amish were granted exemption from the plan. In terms of social insurance programs, all Canadian Amish now have social insurance numbers but their digits are such that they cannot be used to receive and benefits (Nolt, 1992). The story of the Ontario chapter, like its American counterpart, has meant a great deal of interaction with government over such issues as education, pensions, milk storage, worker's compensation, jury duty and selection of cemeteries (Thomson, 1993). For the Amish, it seems, an ever-increasing involvement with the state has become a way of life.

The Amish in Ontario have also revealed a much closer tie with their Mennonite cousins in Ontario than has been the case before. Previously, the Amish lived a completely segregated life, including no involvement with other Anabaptist groups. In Waterloo County the degree of interaction between Amish and Old Order (conservative) Mennonites has been substantial. The two communities have cooperated a great deal in two primary areas: first, in making representations to government on such matters as peace witness, social security and hospitalization; and, second, in matters of mutual aid in times of disaster from fire, floods or violent storms (Fretz, 1989). There are subtle but significant ways in which the Amish in Waterloo County differ from conservative Mennonites (sometimes called "Old Order Mennonites"). Old Order Mennonite men are usually clean-shaven, while Amish men wear beards but no moustaches. Amish women wear dresses that match Mennonite dresses in style but their colors are brighter, using primarily the colors of purple, green and bright blue. Amish use the hook-and eye form of fasteners on their clothing while Mennonites use buttons. There are also slight differences in buggy construction (Epp, 1994). It takes a trained eye to catch these distinctions, but insiders have no difficulty with them. In the meantime, the two communities do cooperate on some matters and this extra political clout helps when their special traits are under fire. In the meantime one can possibly conclude that if coopera-tive with outsiders, even Mennonites, is an indication of the widening lifespace of the Amish, then the process of outside interaction has truly begun.

Cultural Change

Change and Changemakers

Cultural change can take many forms, such as the impact of new technologies or new economic practices. Cultural change can often be subtle and limited, unbeknownst to the particular group involved. Cultural change often occurs by accumulation, and follows the principle of continuity, that is, innovations build on old established foundations.

Cross-fertilization may also occur, new ideas being associated with values already held. Other reasons why cultures change may have to do with knowledge increase, demand of the constituency, the advance of technology or related matters such as the existence of materials. All of these factors may be identified in the Amish community. Cultural change may also come about because of the role of changemakers, individuals or groups who deliberately or inadvertently strive for change in society. The Amish have a name for people who constantly try to stretch the boundaries outlined by the church; they call them "fence jumpers" or "fence crowders". These individuals usually know just how far to go in trying to get a new gadget accepted by the *Ordnung*, so they obtain the item, and if church officials complain they may put it away for a little while until the pressure dies down. In some instances tractors have been recalled from the fields and bathrooms have been torn out, only to be permitted two decades later (Kraybill, 1990).

Wood and Jackson (1982) describe the changemakers of society in terms of three types—reformist, radical and counter movements, the latter which would apply easily to the Amish community. While their "counter" activities have been anything but boisterous for the most part, they have silently but effectively lived a separate lifestyle in North America, unaffected by the larger community except in instances where the latter has impinged upon their chosen lifestyle. Counter movements usually involve direct confrontations to make change, primarily targeting legislative changes. On the matter of schooling the Amish have been more direct by agitating for and gaining approval from government officials to operate parochial schools.

Descriptors of Culture Change

Woods (1974) has suggested that cultural change involving two cultures is largely dependent on the duration and intensity of contact between the two groups. Change through cultural borrowing is greater among groups which have the same cultural inventory, and when it occurs, change commonly proceeds in both directions; both groups influence one another and borrow from one another. Similarly, when change occurs it may also be noted that change produces change. Change to one cultural component may affect change in others. When a particular item is borrowed, it is often modified or its function is reinterpreted to suit local needs. Some parts of a cultural inventory are more resistant to change than others, particularly those related to the underlying value system or *Weltanschauung*. All of these factors apply to the Amish situation.

Despite appearances to the contrary, the Amish community *does* change and adapt to change and this process has occurred in tandem with transformations in the dominant American society. That relationship stretches over two centuries and has been highlighted by a series of intense interconnections and interdependencies. Reciprocal borrowing between the two segments of American society has been significant. The Amish have extensively utilized the benefits of advanced technology and society generally has adapted a wide range of Amish themes also typical of colonial America for commercial purposes. A trip to Amish country will quickly overwhelm the tourist with the wide variety of Amish-like goods for sale, some of them even manufactured in foreign countries. The principle that change produces change is evident in Amish adaptations to technology, for example, their acceptance of 110-volt electrical devices through the use of adapters. Amish structures, houses, barns and industrial buildings also reveal the effect of modern engineering.

Cultural Lag Theory

The proposition that elements of culture are more resistant to change than others, originated in Ogburn's (1922) theory of cultural lag. Ogburn postulated that society consists of two interdependent systems called material and non-material, or technology and value system. A value system is most widely and firmly held when it is in harmony with the material facts in the technological system. The gist of Ogburn's theory is that culture in general, including institutional life, is constantly changing and faced with the challenge of keeping values caught up to the more rapidly changing technological elements to which they unavoidably have reference. Ogburn's theory has been criticized on the basis that technological change is not necessarily always ahead of value change, but values may change independently of, as well as in response to, institutional changes in technology.

Ogburn's theory helps explain change in Amish society, rooted as it is in the traditional mode that values have priority over and govern the extent to which technological advances may be utilized by members of the society. Every societal innovation contemplated for use by an Amish individual must be approved by the local *Ordnung*. That body does not have to offer any explanation for its approval or disapproval of an application, but simply decree whether or not the device or practice in question is in violation of established principles. Maintaining long-established principles is of utmost importance, and a long list of criteria by which to evaluate innovations is used by the *Ordnung* in making a decision. These include: economic impact, visibility, ties to sacred symbols, linkage to profane symbols, limitations, external influence, ostentatious display, and possible damage to family solidarity (Kraybill, 1990). The potential advantage which the innovation might hold is irrelevant. Members of the *Ordnung* need not deliberate long, and their decision is final, no matter how ridiculous it may appear to outsiders or, if negative, how disappointing it may be to the membership.

Conclusion

The Amish alternative to full participation in the dominant societal social system has been subject to its share of ups and downs over the past two centuries. There are signs that a measure of tolerance towards divergence is a reality in North America. Certainly government actions exempting the Amish from participation in the compulsory social security program and legislation allowing them to operate private schools are indications of a favorable attitude toward Amish. These developments have reduced the pressure on the Plain People. In addition, the current concern for multicultural toleration and advancement of the diversity manifest both in Canada and the United States can only serve to create a more favorable and tolerant public attitude toward the notion of appreciating diversity—which includes the Amish. The tendency for the Amish community to diversify (some would call it splintering) further contributes toward and guarantees the longevity of the group because they can still maintain a basic Amish social order even as they continue to tolerate divergence in their own community. The toleration and concern manifested toward the Amish by more "worldly" Anabaptist groups can similarly be a positive factor in helping the Plain People to maintain their identity. There are several instances where more liberal Mennonite groups, such as the Mennonite Central Committee have gone to bat to assist the Amish with legal problems. While this kind of assistance may be appreciated by the Amish, it is never solicited. As most former Amish people will probably testify, the role of the Amish is to demonstrate that the preservation of an ideal culminates in the living out of that ideal. When that ideal is the pursuit of the simple life, avoiding conflict and doing an honest day's work, it represents one of the most vitally-needed principles of our time.

Today's Amish will struggle with many of the same forms of social malaise that North Americans face. They will seek to conquer them with the resources of the church,

Figure 8-3. Amish farm.

family, community, schooling and, believe it or not, what may appear to be social science-inspired insights. These insights are evidenced from time to time in issues of the Canadian Amish publication, *Family Life*, produced in Ontario. In a section of the magazine devoted to domestic issues, several letters to the editor indicate the same degree of concern about aberrations in Amish family life as in any North American family. Parents express concern about their children, and Amish woman complain that their husbands are not attentive enough. One woman, expressed the pain she experienced when her husband made fun of her attempts to lose weight. In her letter she suggested that if husbands were more affectionate toward their wives, the latter might do more to please them. Nagging a wife is no substitute for kindness and sensitivity. As she put it, "If they [wives] would get all the love they need from their husbands, they wouldn't keep trying to fill that void within themselves with food. If supplying this affection is too much trouble for the husbands, they can just forget about voicing their opinions about that extra fat" (*Family Life*, n.d.). It would appear, then, that the same basic social conflicts that are manifest in greater society are also in existence among the Amish.

Cultural trappings can temporarily disguise the twentieth-century perplexities brought about by increased technology and decreased social sensitivity. The fact that the Amish recognize, like anyone else, that their way of life has been infiltrated by many of the disintegrative factors of modern civilization is a good indication that they are in many ways living in this age. A first impression of them will appear otherwise, but a second look will clearly indicate the extent to which they have managed to synthesize many of the basic institutions in their social network—home, school and church. The functional aspects of their way of life far outweigh the dysfunctional components, like the apparent generation gap, and constitute a good indication that their society will endure. In this sense, the Amish may be the best proof yet that North American multiculturalism can be a functional concept.

References

Epp, Marlene. (1994). *Mennonites in Ontario*. St. Jacobs, ON: The Mennonite Historical Society of Ontario.

Fretz, J. Winfield. (1989). *The Waterloo Mennonites: A Community in Paradox*. Waterloo, ON: Wilfred Laurier Press.

Gingerich, Orland. (1972). *The Amish of Canada*. Waterloo, ON: Conrad Press.

Hochstetler, Martin and Susan Hochstetler. (1991). *Cabin Life on the Kootenai*. West Union, OH: Published by the authors.

Hostetler, John A. (1993). *Amish Society*. fourth edition. Baltimore, MD: The Johns Hopkins University Press.

Klimuska, Ed. (1993). The Amish are Changing. *Lancaster New Era*, Tuesday, July 20, A10.

Kraybill, Donald B. (1990). *The Riddle of Amish Culture.* Baltimore, MD: The Johns Hopkins University Press.

Nolt, Steven M. (1992). *A History of the Amish.* Intercourse, PA: Good Books.

Ogburn, William F. (1922). *Social Change.* New York: B. W. Huebsch Inc.

Regehr, T. D. (1993). The Experience of the Old Order Amish in Canada after 1940. Unpublished Paper. Saskatoon, SK: The University of Saskatchewan.

Schreiber, William I. (1990). *Our Amish Neighbors.* Wooster, OH: Wooster College Press.

Thomson, Dennis B. (1993). Canadian Government Relations. *The Amish and the State.* Donald B. Kraybill, ed. Baltimore, MD: The Johns Hopkins University Press, 235–250.

Wood, James L. and Maurice Jackson, eds (1982). *Social Movements: Development, Participation and Dynamics.* Belmont, CA: Wadsworth.

Woods, Clyde M. (1974). *Culture Change.* Dubuque, IA: William C. Brown.

Zook, Noah. (1988). *Seeking a Better Country.* seventh edition. Gordonville, PA: Gordonville Print Shop.

Index

Subject Index